Gabe's Guide to Budget Travel

Travel Tips, Tricks, Things to Bring and Places to Go

By Gabriel Morris

Visit the author's website for more info:
Gabrieltraveler.com

Table of Contents

Chapter 12. *Greece and the Greek Isles*

Mainland: Athens, Delphi, Meteora, Mt. Olympus, Pelion Peninsula; Greek   Isles: Santorini, Rhodes, Anafi, Milos, Patmos, Lipsi, Leros, Nisyros, Naxos,   Aegina

Chapter 13. *Turkey*

Istanbul, Pamukkale, Termessos, Kabak, Oludeniz, Lycian Way trek, Cappadocia

Chapter 14. *Egypt*

Cairo, Great Pyramids, Aswan, Luxor, Dakhla Oasis, Bahariya Oasis

Chapter 15. *Thailand*

Bangkok, Ayutthaya, Chiang Mai, Pai, Ko Mak, Ko Kood, Ko Phayam

Chapter 16. *The Philippines*

Palawan Island: Puerto Princesa, Sabang, El Nido

Chapter 17. *Nepal*

Pokhara, Annapurna Base Camp trek

Chapter 18. *Singapore*

Introduction.

My first budget travel trip abroad began the day after my 18th birthday, May 1990, when I flew from San Francisco, California to London, England to begin a 4-month backpacking trip around Europe. I visited 10 countries altogether. I hitchhiked the length of the U.K. across England, Wales, Scotland and northern Ireland, slept out on the streets of Paris, explored the Greek Isles, climbed Mt. Olympus, camped in the Alps, hitchhiked through the Pyrenees and more.

I didn't take another trip outside of the U.S. until the end of that decade. I started university in Alaska, worked in Denali National Park for the summers, moved back to California for a semester, moved to Oregon where a friend lived to continue my college education there; and then effectively dropped out for the next five years or so. I hitchhiked around the western U.S., worked on farms, worked again in Alaska, attended festivals, lived on communes, lived in the Hawaiian rainforest for several months, and more. I was pretty much the proverbial rolling stone.

In the fall of 1999 I flew to India for five months. Upon returning from that trip, I didn't travel abroad for another six years, as I settled into a fairly normal life for a change, living and working in Portland, Oregon. In 2005 the travel bug hit me again, and I was off to India for another 3-month adventure during the winter of 2005-2006. Since then, I've spent a good chunk of every year traveling. In 2007-

2008 I spent 8 months in Hawaii, Thailand, India and Nepal. In 2009 I spent 4 ½ months in Greece, Egypt and Turkey. And in 2010-2011 I spent 5 months in the Philippines, Malaysia, Singapore and India (for the 4th time). I also worked in Jasper National Park, Canada during three different stints between 2008 and 2011.

So, that's my budget traveling background. Altogether I've spent 27 months traveling abroad (not including my years vagabonding around the U.S., or working in Canada). People often ask me how I've managed to travel so much and for such long stretches of time, since I don't have a high-paying job, a trust fund, an inheritance or any other steady source of cash coming in.

In this book I will answer that question based on my own personal experiences, and provide much more useful information as well: from buying a plane ticket and planning out your itinerary, to packing for your trip, tips for saving money while traveling; as well as a guide to my favorite places in some of the most interesting countries that I've been to.

The book is organized in the same order as you would proceed with your trip, starting with the first question—Where should I go?? Once you figure that out, it's all about finding a cheap flight. Then, you'll want to plan out an itinerary (or maybe not!). You get the idea. So grab a map, turn the page and let's start brainstorming for the travel plans!

Part 1: Preliminary Preparations

Chapter 1—*Where should I go?*

This is, of course, a big question that could entail volumes of information about all the different countries of the world. I'm just going to give you a few tips (for now) on narrowing things down based on various criteria. Most likely, you already have a few ideas in mind of places you've read about, seen photos or brochures of, heard about through friends who have visited certain countries, etc. And of course, for some additional ideas, read through Part 2 of this book in which I give reviews of my favorite places in some of the most interesting countries I've been to.

But basically, you're going to want to put the feelers out there and start narrowing things down a bit, and/or learning about some new places. One of the most important considerations is, of course, your budget. This book, as the title implies, will focus on budget travel. However, there is a bit of a range in that category. Some might consider staying in 2 and 3 star hotels budget travel. Others are thinking more along the lines of my first backpacking trip to Europe, stretching the few dollars they have as far as possible, and are willing to put up with some very minimal conditions in order to achieve that goal. This book will be tackling things from a general perspective that should prove helpful to both those who simply want an affordable week's vacation to the Greek isles, for example; as well as those who want to spend several years backpacking around the world.

One of the first things you'll need to do is get some sort of general grasp on how much your daily expenses will be in any given country. If you've already determined how much *time* you have to travel, and know how much *money* you will have available, then do a quick calculation and figure out, roughly, how much per day you can afford to spend.

Now, if you do that calculation and come up with, say, $40, then you can already narrow things down quite a bit. Don't get discouraged, however, if that number (or whatever number you arrive at) looks rather paltry! Because that amount, and even less than that, will actually go a VERY LONG WAYS in some countries, depending of course on how you travel.

Just to give you an idea, during my first, 5-month trip to India in 1999-2000, I figured out afterwards that overall I had spent an average of $8.50/day. No, that is not a typo, and the decimal is in the correct place! And no, this did not entail sleeping out on the streets at all, begging, living in an ashram, or even being ridiculously tight with my money. This included having a hotel room to myself most of the time (except a few times when I shared a room with someone I'd met while traveling), eating 2-3 meals a day in restaurants, buying new clothes, etc. for myself as well as gifts for friends and family, and even mailing back a package of stuff. India, and much of Asia, is just ridiculously cheap thanks to the power of the American dollar (or the

Euro, British Pound, etc.). Granted, this was 12 years ago, prices have gone up and the last few times I went to India I spent more like $12-15 a day. But still, as you can see, it is very possible to travel to certain places in the world on much less than you might have expected.

So let's say that you have $40 a day to work with. And let's say that some of the countries on your list are: **Sweden**, **France**, **Greece**, **Thailand, the Philippines**, **India** and **Egypt**, just for some examples. Now, how do you plan to travel? If you're not one who enjoys sleeping in a tent, then right away you can cross Sweden, France and Greece off your list. I haven't actually been to Sweden, but it's certainly one of the most expensive countries in the world. France isn't far behind, and though Greece is cheaper by comparison, since they're using the Euro (although who knows for how much longer) prices are still in line with much of the rest of Europe.

When I visited Greece for the first time in 1990, I stayed in a hostel on the island of Santorini for about $3. When I re-visited Greece in 2009, hostel prices had skyrocketed and were roughly $25, about the same as in the U.S. If you have only $40 a day to spare, even if you were to stay in hostels, that doesn't leave hardly anything left over for everything else you will have to spend your hard-earned money on. However, remember the qualifier—*if you're willing to camp, that changes things.* I spent three months in Greece in 2009, and my budget overall was actually just a little over $30 per day. I'll talk more about how I was able to do that later.

So here's what I would suggest first—go to a bookstore sometime when you have a few hours or an afternoon free, and find their travel guidebooks section. Then grab the guidebooks for several countries that you're interested in, take a seat on the floor or in a chair and start perusing. You may also come across some countries in the process that you hadn't thought of. Bring a pen and notebook along so that you can write some things down. As you look through the books, there are some indicators you can jot down that will give you a basic idea of your daily budget in that country.

Personally, I recommend the **Rough Guides**. For one, they tend to pack more pages into their guidebooks, which means more information and more places. This is important because, as I'll discuss later, one of the keys to traveling is to find those out-of-the-way spots that, for mysterious reasons, haven't attracted much attention, even though they may be one of the most interesting or beautiful places in the country. Every country has these places. But it may take a bit of work to find them. This will give you something to do in the months leading up to your trip. Some of my favorite places in India, for example, were only given a few paragraphs or so in the Rough Guide...but weren't even mentioned at all in the **Lonely Planet** guidebook for India. I did notice however that the newest editions of Rough Guide and Lonely Planet for India have roughly the same number of pages, so perhaps Lonely Planet has beefed up all their books a bit.

So pick a budget-leaning guidebook, whether it be the Rough Guides, Lonely Planet, Moon Handbooks, Let's Go or another one. Scan through it, check out the photos, read some excerpts here and there to get a little more acquainted with the country. And, **WRITE DOWN SOME NUMBERS**. For example, how much is a basic hotel room? That number alone will give you a good idea right away of what things cost there. In the Lonely Planet books, for example, they generally divide the accommodations section for each city into three sections for the different budgets, i.e. budget, mid-range and high end. If you're hoping to stay in 2 and 3 star hotels, write down a few prices from the mid-range section. If you're intending to travel as cheaply as possible, write down the cheapest prices you see in the budget section.

If it's quoted in Euros or Rupees or Baht, or whatever foreign currency and you're not in the mood to look through the book trying to find the exchange rates (especially considering they may have changed), then write down the number in that currency for now (I'll provide a currency exchange website with the latest rates, just below). Then, if you're willing to stay in hostels, write down the amount for a bed in a hostel, or for a private room. If you're willing to camp, find a campground or two in the book and write down how much they charge. These numbers will give you an idea of whether or not you can afford to go there.

When you get back home with your list of assorted prices in various currencies, get online and visit **http://www.xe.com**, which is a website with up-to-the-minute currency rates, where you can calculate the exchange rates for different currencies, so that you have a real number in mind that you can work with. (Note that these exchange rates are variable based on a variety of factors, and you may get a slightly different rate once you're actually inside the country.)

If your budget is $40 and you've figured out that your preferred accommodation is $30, that doesn't leave much left to cover all the other expenses of eating, transportation, entry fees to events and attractions, gifts, random unexpected expenditures, etc. If your preferred accommodation is $20 or less, however, that gives you a little more wiggle room, especially if you're prepared to be tight with your budget in other areas. And it also says that that particular country is on the cheap side, so other things will be cheaper as well. In Turkey I was able to find private rooms in that price range. In India, I've stayed in rooms that were literally as cheap as $1. And you can easily expect to spend less than $5 for a private hotel room in India on a regular basis. Even in Thailand I had great little bamboo huts right on a beautiful beach for $5 or so.

Another online resource I'll recommend is the **Lonely Planet Thorn Tree forum**. It's a free discussion forum on the Lonely Planet guidebooks website, in which people ask travel questions and then others come along and provide answers:

http://www.lonelyplanet.com/thorntree/index.jspa

This is a great addendum to whichever guidebook you might end up getting, because it provides more current, personalized, on-the-ground information about a particular place. It's organized by country, so you can scroll down the list on that page, select a specific country and then see what people are talking about. For example, if there's a revolution going on there that hasn't made mainstream news headlines, you might want to know about that! Or a recent earthquake, typhoon, general strike, etc. But beyond that, it will also give you another window into that particular country. You can simply scan through the different threads that people have posted recently to see what people are talking about; use the search function to find information about something in particular (i.e. plug in "Greek isles daily budget" or "Thailand best beaches") and there's probably a discussion thread or two somewhere that will address that. Or, sign up for a free account and then post your own question, and see if you get some helpful feedback.

So hopefully this first chapter gives you just a very general idea of how to get started. Later on I will be discussing many of these same subjects more in-depth. Essentially, you want to start soaking up some more information about different areas you're interested in, in order to get a more realistic, practical idea of whether or not it's really where you want to go, beyond the cliches and mystique surrounding certain places based on promotional efforts, ancient history and who knows what else. For example, I visited 13 different Greek isles between my two trips there. Everyone has heard of Rhodes, and its famous Collosus, right? (If not, it was a huge statue erected there around 300 BC, and one of the original seven Wonders of the World.) Well, Rhodes was without a doubt my *least* favorite Greek isle.

You don't want to spend your hard-earned money and precious time somewhere based on rumors, past glory or promotional posters that may or may not give an accurate idea of what the area is really like today. It's worth taking the time and doing some homework in the months before your trip to learn more about the places that are must-sees; the places that are pure hype and just going to be a tourist circus without much worth seeing; and especially those places that sound intriguing based on perhaps only a paragraph or two in the guidebook, or one person's passionate testimony read somewhere online, and which sounds worth visiting yourself to find out in person. My favorite places are very often those out-of-the-way spots that come as a welcomed surprise and a break from the popular tourist trail. And finding those places is half the fun.

Chapter 2—*Buying a flight*

So, you've figured out where you actually want to go (or perhaps you've just picked a single destination and will be winging it from there, which is perfectly fine...as long as you keep a few things in mind). Congratulations! Now, it's time to buy a flight.

Unfortunately, there is no single website or sure-fire way to get the cheapest flight. Flight prices fluctuate constantly, and there's no way of knowing whether, if you wait another day or week or month, the price will then be higher or lower than whatever you're seeing at the moment. So I'll just pass on a few ideas that I've found useful over the years, and then it'll be a matter of scanning the different websites and finding the best price. Just plug in "budget flights" or "cheap tickets" into your preferred search engine and start clicking and searching.

Personally, I've found Expedia.com to consistently have the best deals overall, so I've used them more than any other online flight booking service. However, things change quickly in both the online world and the airlines business. One important tip is, when it comes to flights in a particular region, there may very well be much better deals using local carriers. Air Asia (**http://www.airasia.com**) has amazing deals on flights all around Asia. Recently I was comparing flights from Bangkok, Thailand to New Delhi, India. **Expedia.com** was showing around $250 for a one-way flight. *Air Asia had a flight on the very same day for $75*. I was able to hop around the islands of the

Philippines using local carriers such as Air Phil Express and Cebu Pacific for as little as $25 for an hour-long flight. And the same was the case for short flights within Turkey. So it may very well save you a pile of money to book different legs of your trip using different airlines purchased separately, rather than just plugging your itinerary into Expedia or whatever online book site, and taking the cheapest thing they offer.

The brilliant thing about travel nowadays, is that you don't get totally screwed purchasing one-way flights. Oftentimes, the cost for two separate one-way flights is almost the same as the two-way flight. And in 2009 when I was looking at flights to Greece, the one-way flight from San Francisco to Athens was actually a little *less* than half the cost of the two-way flight (in other words, cheaper to buy two one-way flights than one round-trip flight).

So with that in mind, if you're gearing up for a months-long journey and perhaps not sure how far your money will go, or even where exactly you will want to go, then it's a great idea to simply leave the trip open-ended. Buy a one-way flight to your first destination and then, once you decide it's time to move on—either back home or to another country—you can start scanning for flights then and you'll certainly find something. However, you WILL want to factor in a cushion of a few hundred dollars, because it is of course possible that flights may go up, ESPECIALLY if you may be flying during the holiday season, or high season for that particular area. So there is a bit of a risk to leaving things open-ended. But, it is equally possible that prices may actually go down rather than up. As long as you can afford to take the chance, it's a very worthwhile chance to take.

And by the way, the European equivalent to Air Asia would be Ryan Air (**http://www.ryanair.com/en**). I haven't actually used them before; but based on what I've heard from others they are pretty much the cheapest airline out there. And another basic tip: **whenever possible when booking flights, always pick a Tuesday or Wednesday to fly, as they are almost always cheaper than other days of the week.** *While looking at flights from Hawaii to India recently, the difference between the flight on a Wednesday, and the exact same flight two days later on a Friday, was $600!*

One important thing that needs to be mentioned here if you do choose the "winging it" route—or if you buy an assortment of flights from different websites and airlines—*is that certain countries don't allow one-way flights into them.* You will want to research this beforehand so that you don't get yourself into a bind. This could be a great question to ask on the Lonely Planet forum. Because it may be that although some countries technically might not allow it, they never actually check; whereas other countries that don't allow it might be more strict about it.

As an example, when I flew to the Philippines in 2010, before even boarding the flight in San Francisco the airlines asked for proof of an onward flight, because I was using a one-way ticket. I did have an onward flight, but it was with a different airline on a different ticket. I didn't have a print out of it handy, not anticipating that they would have a problem with it. So they asked me to come into the office behind the check-in desk with one of the attendants, get online on one of their computers and log into my email account, so that I could show them proof of my onwards departure. That proved sufficient and I was able to board my flight without any further delays.

Now, there are a few other ways to deal with this situation. One is that, if you've done your research and figured out that, well, other travelers are saying they've flown to such-and-such country regularly without an onward flight, even though technically their rules state that it isn't allowed...then the chances of them making an issue of it is minimal. So you could go ahead with the one-way flight, **WITH SOME ADDITIONAL RESEARCH AS A BACK-UP PLAN**. Because if they do stop you and say that they need proof of a flight to another destination, you can solve that on the spot if you have enough time—by simply going online and purchasing a flight then and there, and then showing them the proof. But, you obviously don't want to be starting from scratch in this case, which will take time and more than likely cost you money. So, find the various options for places to fly to sometime in the days or weeks before your flight, the best deals, etc., so that if that situation arises you can deal with it smoothly, not miss your flight and not spend a bunch of money unnecessarily.

And by the way, this is a good point at which to mention something fairly obvious, but which bears repeating—**ARRIVE EARLY TO YOUR FLIGHTS!** It's much better to have a couple of extra hours to kill, reading a book or surfing online at the airport, than to be sweating bullets in the taxi or in the security line, because you cut things a bit too close.

Now, one other option for dealing with the one-way flights scenario, is to make use of carriers such as Air Asia, and purchase a dirt cheap ticket out of the country that you're flying into, purely so that you can show them that you have proof of onward travel. For example, my ticket from Manila, Philippines to Kota Kinabalu, on the island of Borneo in Malaysia, was ridiculously cheap. I don't remember exactly how much at the time. But just now, January 2012, I checked that same flight on Airasia.com for a one-way flight next month. And it's only $38!

So it's an option to simply purchase a flight out of a country, purely so that you can then be able show them, either when you check-in for your first flight or else when going through customs in the destination country, that you have that onward ticket, whether or not you intend to use it. And of course, it makes sense to pick that flight as a destination that you might want to head to anyway, so that it's more likely to get used. But if you don't use it, $40 then isn't much of a loss in the grand scheme of your trip, especially if it insures that you won't have to tangle with the authorities.

Another possible way to go is to book an **around-the-world flight**, which very well could save you some money. One website I've used previously is **http://www.around-the-world.com**. Or just plug in "around the world flights" and do a bit of searching. This would, of course, be the other end of the spectrum from winging it. And if you want to visit multiple destinations, it could very well be the cheapest way to do so. At least you will know exactly what you're going to pay on your flights, and won't have any surprises along your trip with the possibility of prices jumping northward.

Just to give you a rough idea, you can most likely find an around-the-world flight (or multiple destination, which might not literally go around the world but which will bring you back to your place of departure) that incorporates 4-7 different stops, for $2,000-$3,000, and quite possibly even less. These would most likely be a predetermined package, that wouldn't give you the flexibility of switching them around will-nilly. But considering that you could easily spend that much on a simple round-trip flight to a lot of places, this could be a great option to go with.

Chapter 3—*Planning your itinerary*

Now, I can't say that I will be basing this chapter on personal experience—because I never plan out an itinerary! However, I can still offer a few suggestions. The first goes back to simply figuring out where you actually want to go. And again I would highly recommend reading through a guidebook well, specifically so that you can find out about those out-of-the-way spots. Once you've decided on your destination or destinations, it would be a good idea to head back down to the bookstore, and pick up one of the guidebooks there. And if you've come up with a few places that sound intriguing and which you want to learn more about, bring that list along. Then, check what they have to say in several different books. It's quite possible they will have slightly, or even wildly different perspectives on the same place. By getting a few different points of view, you might get a little better idea as to whether that place is still worth investigating—or else whether you should cross it off the list of places to visit.

The last time I visited India, for example, I did indeed have a list of half a dozen or so places that I wanted to go to, based on a combination of having heard about them through the grapevine on previous trips to India, reading a little about them online and then perusing the guidebooks. And I did map out a general course that would take them into account with the least amount of wasted traveling time, since it isn't easy covering large distances in India. So I am by no means against itineraries. For one thing, this was in the course of a four-month trip there, so I had plenty of time to work with. If you're only going on a week-long vacation, or a few weeks, then you will of course be more inclined towards planning things out beforehand.

My number one suggestion for planning an itinerary would be **DON'T TRY TO CRAM IN TOO MUCH**. It all depends, of course, on what sort of vacation you're looking forward to. If your number one priority is simply to see as much as you can possibly see, then by all means, go for it. However, as for myself, I don't want to spend an inordinate amount of my traveling time sitting on buses and trains, in airports, etc. I want plenty of time to really soak up a place. On that recent trip to India, I spent a month in one place, and two weeks in another. I'll often spend at least a week somewhere, assuming it's worth staying there of course. I would rather have free time to get acquainted with a place, connect a bit with the locals, get a genuine sense for it, be able to explore winding alleys, go on nearby hikes, learn about some places that only the locals know about, etc.

For example, on that trip to India, I ended up visiting a temple that I'd heard about from a local I was talking to in a shared jeep taxi on my way to my guest house (this was in the **Himalaya mountains** of

Uttarakhand State, west of **Nepal**). The temple wasn't mentioned in my guidebook. But I was able to find out where it was online and with some further help from locals. It involved taking a bus, getting off at the right place, and then hiking about a mile up a dirt road that wound past local villagers' houses. And then, voila!, there was this amazing, ancient stone temple commanding a spectacular view over the whole valley. The only other people there were some workers who were doing some renovations on it. The point being, not every interesting site or attraction is necessarily covered in a guidebook. There are still relatively undiscovered places out there.

Now, if you do indeed have only a week or two, and you're making hotel reservations, train reservations, etc. beforehand, then of course you will need to plan out your itinerary day-by-day. Again, I would simply suggest to narrow things down so that you aren't trying to do too much. If you've heard about several different places that you want to go to, and two of them are on opposite sides of a country, then it would probably be a good idea to take a good hard look and decide to cross one of the places off the list, rather than going way out of your way and spending precious time getting there, if you have limited time. There will always be interesting places that you won't get to see. Try not to focus too much on the number of places that you see on your trip, and instead focus on the overall experience of enjoying immersing yourself in the rhythm of a country.

If you're going to the **Greek isles** for ten days, do you really need to see a new island every day or two? If you're on a cruise, that's one thing. But if it's a matter of catching ferries, flights, buses, taxis, etc. each time you change islands, why not just pick two or three, and have more time to explore the places you're going? Again, this is where it pays to do your reading beforehand, so that you end up somewhere you definitely want to be. Each Greek isle is unique and has different things to offer (even if I wasn't a fan of Rhodes, it was still worth visiting and seeing how it compared to the other islands). Some of the ones you hear about the most are the least enjoyable ones to visit, and some of the ones you never hear about at all are the best ones to visit. I'll explore the Greek isles much more in-depth in Part 2 of the book.

But in short, just keep in mind that when traveling, the towns and sights and attractions that you hear about most often, are by no means the only places you should focus on in your research. Yes, read about them, for one so that you can hopefully figure out if the reality actually matches up to the hype. But read and research beyond those places. Doing so will almost certainly give you a much richer, more interesting and probably even more relaxing traveling experience, when you aren't spending your entire trip fighting the tourist crowds.

Chapter 4—*Booking hotel rooms*

One essential consideration related to planning out your itinerary is, of course, booking hotels and hostels. For the most part, I don't book rooms in advance, precisely because I don't plan out a day-by-day itinerary. I want to keep my plans and options open, so that I can go wherever I feel like on a whim, based on learning about a place in the course of my trip, doing more reading of places along the way, perhaps even just hopping off a bus or train somewhere at random that looks interesting. And in all the traveling I've done, I've never been stuck without a room...*oh, wait, that isn't entirely true!*

Remember in the Introduction, I mentioned something about sleeping out on the streets of Paris? Okay, so that was the one time. It was towards the end of my trip, and I arrived in Paris with very little money left. I went to a booking office that I'd used previously (I passed through Paris three different times during my 1990 Europe trip) and all of the hostels were full up. I think there was a cheap hotel room available for $40; which now of course sounds like the deal of the century. But at the time I was only camping or staying in hostels, and $40 was a good chunk of what I had left for my final week in Europe. So I spent the night sleeping on the Pont Neuf bridge across the River Seine. If you're curious how that turned out, check out my new book *Following My Thumb: A Decade of Unabashed Wanderlust*. In short, not so good! But at least it made an interesting story.

So anyway, when it comes to Paris, London, Athens and other big cities, it is of course recommended to book something in advance, especially if you'll be arriving at the end of a long flight, and *ESPECIALLY* if you're flying in in the evening or middle of the night. It depends to some extent, however, on which big city. If there's a "backpacker's area" of the city, i.e. a concentration of cheap hotels and hostels in one particular neighborhood, such as the Paharganj disctrict in Delhi, or Khao San Road in Bangkok, then you can easily get away with simply showing up and then checking out different places until you find somewhere that both suits your expectations of comfort, as well as your budget.

The advantage to doing it this way, is that you won't be deceived by photos on a website that might misrepresent a particular establishment, or otherwise find yourself disappointed with your room, or simply the mattress. You can take a look in person, check out the room, shower, mattress, the hotel restaurant, friendliness of the clientele, etc. before handing over your money. The downside is that you might end up spending a bit of time going from one place to the next before you find something adequate. If it's the middle of the day, you've got the energy and patience to do so, and the different hotels aren't too far apart, then this can be a good way to go. Otherwise, booking in advance, at least for your first night or two, is probably a better idea.

Now, hotel room prices (other than hostel bunks) can fluctuate almost as much as flights. I actually worked at the front desk of a hotel in Jasper National Park, Canada for two summers and was the night auditor, looking over all the assorted bills. So I saw how wildly different the charges were from one person to the next. I also was allowed to charge walk-in guests (people without reservations) at my discretion based on what I thought they might be able to afford (and then I received commission for charging a higher price). So, I know first-hand that hotel room prices can vary considerably. Some people were paying literally two to three times as much as others, for the same type of room on the same night.

That being said, if you are booking in advance you'll want to search around for prices online the same as if you were searching for a flight, because you will find different prices on different websites, on different dates, etc. One important thing to keep in mind, if you're truly looking for the cheapest room but don't want to stay in a shared accommodation situation such as a bunk in a hostel, is that hostels oftentimes have private rooms, which are much cheaper than hotels. Take a look at the hostel websites such as **http://www.hostels.com**, **http://www.hostelworld.com**, **http://www.hostelbookers.com/hostels**, etc. You will almost certainly find a much cheaper room there than elsewhere. And a big advantage to staying in a hostel, is that you'll be mingling with fellow budget travelers and have a good chance of meeting someone new. If you're traveling alone, who knows, maybe you'll meet someone to travel with! And of course, the quickest and easiest way to bring down a room price is to split it 50/50 with someone else.

Chapter 5—*Getting your passport and visa*

I have one main suggestion when it comes to dealing with passports and visas: do it earlier, rather than later! There's nothing worse than counting down your final week or two before your flight, waiting for that passport or visa to arrive in the mail, wondering if you should have done it a month earlier. This was the case with my first trip to India. My Indian visa arrived a day or two before my flight. Too close for comfort!

Now the second suggestion, regarding visas, is to read the rules closely, as they can be rather convoluted. Whichever guidebook you settle on should address visas for that particular country. But sometimes things still aren't clear, and/or you never know when the rules might change. This is another topic in which making use of the Lonely Planet forum, or some other traveler's discussion forum can come in very handy.

As an example, I'll briefly explain the process for visas to **Thailand**, which is really quite confusing. I planned to stay there for seven weeks the first visit, fly to India and Nepal for several months, and then visit Thailand again on the same trip for another month, on my way back. I eventually figured out that there were a couple of ways to go. Thailand allows most foreigners to enter the country for 30 days without a visa. They then allow you to exit the country, and then re-enter right away, for a new 30-day stamp in your passport. However, you *also* have the option of getting a formal visa beforehand, good for 90 days.

Now, I was considering going to **Laos** and/or **Cambodia** on the same trip. So it sounded like I could get away with arriving without a visa, staying for the 30 days, then going to either Laos or Cambodia for however long, and returning for the remainder of my time in Thailand, again without needing a visa. And then for my next return to Thailand after India and Nepal, I would be in the clear since it would be less than 30 days.

However, I wasn't entirely certain about visiting Laos or Cambodia during my first visit. In the course of my research, I discovered there was a Thailand embassy in Portland, where I was living, where you could go in person and get your visa while you waited. I decided it was better to be on the safe side and get the visa beforehand. It was a relief to be able to do it in person, without having to wait for it in the mail. And I was glad that I did—as I never did go to either Laos or Cambodia, so I would have been stuck having to exit the country for a day or two in order to restart another 30-day period.

So in short, do your reading on the subject early in your investigations, rather than leaving it until you have barely enough time to take care of it. Everything else is subject to some degree of flexibility. Passports and visas most likely are not.

One phrase you will likely come across is **"visa on arrival"**. This is precisely what it sounds like. It's pretty much the same thing as the 30-day stamp on arrival when entering Thailand without an official visa, with the exception being that you will have to pay something. When entering both **Egypt** and **Nepal** they offered this "visa on arrival", which was simply a fancier looking stamp than the usual kind, and required paying a fee (which can vary depending on nationality, and may fluctuate over time, so best to check the latest information; but generally it will be in the range of $20-50). The key thing to keep in mind is that a "visa on arrival" doesn't require you to do anything beforehand, other than have a valid passport (and possibly it will need to be valid for a full 6 months from when you are entering the country). You will, however, want to double-check that your home country is included in the list of qualifying countries. **ALSO, you will want to make sure that you are carrying some U.S. cash.** When I entered Nepal (in 2008) *ONLY U.S. CASH WAS ACCEPTED* to pay for the visa at the time. It's a good idea to have some U.S. cash handy anyway, for other similar circumstances that could arrive; or else simply as some back up cash in case you have problems accessing an ATM or changing money at some point.

Chapter 6—*Equipment list*

Woo hoo! So your travels are fast approaching. The flight is booked, you've figured out where you want to go, passport is in hand with the necessary visas, and your trip is only weeks or even days away. Time to start getting packed. First things first, here's a complete list of all the things you *might* want to bring on your travels:

-backpack

-daypack

-sleeping bag/blanket

-rain jacket/rain pants if needed

-warm weather/cold weather clothes (depending on where you're going)

-warm hat/sun hat

-towel

-bandanna

-pocketknife/multi-tool

-sunglasses

-headlamp/flashlight

-camera/tripod/extra memory cards/camera case

-travel guidebook/other reading books

-lighter/matches

-books/journal/pen

-chapstick

-extra batteries/rechargeable batteries

-battery charger

-voltage converter (for converting 110V, in the U.S. and Canada and elsewhere, to 220V in Europe and most countries around the world, or vice versa; *see below for more info on these*)

-socket adapter (so that you can plug your laptop/battery charger/shaver, etc. into one of the different electrical socket types around the world; *again, see below for further explanation*)

-razors/electrical shaver/beard trimmer

-soap/shampoo

-toilet paper

-any necessary medications

-moleskin (for blisters)

-needle/thread

-compact scissors

-cup or small bowl/spoon/spreading knife

-watch/clock

-cell phone

-laptop computer

-journal/notebook/pens

-wallet w/ID, etc.

-fingernail clippers

-playing cards/hacky sack/chess set or other compact game

-snorkel mask/swim goggles/swim fins

-super glue

-several small key/combination locks

-grapefruit seed extract (for dealing with stomach parasites)

-water purifier, such as chlorine dioxide

-bug repellent

-money belt

-ear plugs

-sleeping mask (aka nightshade)

Whew! A long list I know. But most of the items are quite small. I promise, they can all fit into a backpack, with room to spare. Now, despite this long list, remember that this is only a list of *ideas* for what to bring. You'll want to consider every item carefully as to whether or not you actually need it/want it for your particular trip. My number one suggestion in that regard would be: *when in doubt, leave it out!* (With a few essentials that you definitely don't want to leave out, which I'll explain below.)

Budget traveling isn't the same as camping. You aren't going to be on your own in the wilderness, separated from civilization. You can buy stuff when you get there. And if you're going somewhere cheap such as Asia or Africa, you might as well buy at least some of your traveling items, in particular clothes, once you get there and figure out what you actually will and won't need. In the process you'll get some new stuff for cheap, some of which will be great souvenirs to bring back home. And the important thing to keep in mind is this: *you don't want to end up mailing stuff back that it turns out you didn't need.*

For example, when I went to India the first time, in the fall and winter of 1999-2000, I brought my high quality rain jacket. One problem: *winter is the dry season in India.* In five months, I only experienced the faintest of sprinkles once. At some point in my trip I mailed it back, along with a few other items I'd realized I didn't need. This was one of the biggest single expenditures of my entire trip (other than the flight, visa, etc.). For the $50 or so that it cost to mail the stuff back, I could have bought a backpack full of new clothes, or paid for several nights in a fancy hotel, rather than the usual budget places I was staying. And dealing with the post office in foreign countries, particularly in third world countries, is a real hassle that will oftentimes kill most of a day. But I didn't want to carry the jacket around for several more months, and also didn't want to toss it or give it away since it was expensive. I think I included some gifts for family and friends in the package, so that I made some better use of the money spent. But still, it's something you want to avoid having to deal with if possible.

Chapter 7—*Socket adapters and voltage converters*

Now, one of the first things I'll explain that you DEFINITELY DO NOT want to get stuck trying to find in a foreign country is related to electrical items. If you're bringing a digital camera, rechargeable batteries and a battery charger, a cell phone, an electric shaver or beard trimmer, or anything else that you will need to plug into an electrical socket at some point, you will need two very important items (probably, unless the country you're going to is on the same electrical system as your home country).

The first is a *socket adapter*. If you're going to a foreign country that uses a different type of electrical outlet, then your stuff obviously isn't going to plug into their sockets, rendering it all rather useless. So you will need a socket adapter that enables your electrical gadgets to plug into their different sockets. The brilliant thing is that despite there being an assortment of different types of sockets around the world, there is something called a *universal socket adapter*. It allows any type of plug to go into it, and in turn can be plugged into any different type of outlet, thanks to an assortment of different thingies (not sure what else to call them) that either stick out or can be collapsed back into the little contraption, depending on which sort of plug you're dealing with. They're small and lightweight, and you can find them on **Amazon.com** or elsewhere for pretty cheap. Just search for "universal socket adapter"; or else here's one I recommend: the **Insten Universal World Wide Travel Charger Adapter Plug.**

I highly recommend grabbing one of these guys over something that's limited to only one type of socket or plug at either end. Because even if you're only going to one country, you never know if perhaps you might buy an electrical appliance there (such as if you lose your battery charger or something else) and then you'll be able to plug an Indian device, for example, into it (not that you would need to in India of course, but in another country, such as back home). And that way, you'll also be ready to go the next time you travel, perhaps to a different country that uses a different sort of electrical socket.

Now, the second thing that you will most likely need is a *voltage converter*. This is because certain countries, such as the U.S., Canada, much of the Americas, Japan, Taiwan and others, run on 110 volts of electricity (or close to it); whereas other countries such as in Europe, India, Thailand and most of Asia runs on 220 volts (or somewhere in the range from 220-240). The smaller differences between 110 and 120 volts; or else between 220 and 240 don't matter. For example, Thailand runs at 220 volts, and India runs at 230 volts. But you don't need a voltage converter for your appliances from Thailand that you might want to use in India.

However, if you're coming from the U.S. or anywhere else that runs on 110 volts approximately, and you're going to Europe or Asia where it runs on 220-240 volts, you most definitely do need a voltage converter for certain items. Otherwise they will be zapped by the stronger current when you plug them in, and won't work after that.

Now, keep in mind that *certain items are designed specifically to be able to accommodate the full range of voltage from 110-240*—including laptops and cell phones. There's any easy way to confirm whether or not this is the case, just so you can rest easy that you won't end up frying your computer.

On your laptop or cell phone, just check the **AC adapter**. That's the little box in the middle of your power cord for your laptop, with a bunch of itsy-bitsy teeny-weeny writing that you've probably ignored since you bought it (hopefully you didn't remove the label, because you thought it was irrelevant). It's also the plug for your cell phone charger, with similarly tiny, or even smaller writing on the back of it. Depending on your eyesight, you might actually need a magnifying glass in order to read it. Here's what mine says on my laptop power cord:

Input: 100-240V~1A(1A) 50-60Hz

The important thing there is the numbers 100-240V. **That means that it will accept 110 volts, as used in the U.S., as well as 220 volts used in Thailand, 230 volts used in India, etc.** So you're good to go. In this case you DON'T need a voltage converter for your laptop. And although it's almost worn off on my cell phone AC adapter, I can barely read that it says the same thing.

However, not so with my beard trimmer. It reads **Input: 120V**. If I took it to India, plugged it into my fancy new universal socket adapter (as explained above) and then plugged it into the wall, it would be fried and would no longer work. So for that, I do need a voltage converter.

Again, look around Amazon.com or elsewhere, and they aren't too expensive. One caution however: *don't buy the nice and lightweight, cheap ones*. They may only be intended for something such as shaving for ten or fifteen minutes, but NOT for plugging something in to charge for several hours. I had a beard trimmer charger fried due to making this mistake once, and spent the rest of my 8-month trip paying to get my beard trimmed at barbershops around India, Nepal and Thailand...while still hauling around the beard trimmer because I was pretty sure it still worked, and it was just the charger that had gotten fried (which turned out to be the case). So, I would recommend the **Simran SMF-200 Deluxe** (which is currently $13 on Amazon). It's a heavy bugger, but it's compact and will work for whatever device you might end up needing to plug into it.

And in case you're curious or otherwise need to know exactly which countries use which voltage, as well as which type of electrical sockets, this website lists everything for virtually every country in the world:

http://www.kropla.com/electric2.htm

Chapter 8—*More info on things to bring*

Now, on to some of the other items on the list (in Chapter 6) of things to bring.

As far as what sort of carrying bag you might prefer, that's entirely up to you. As I explain in the video above, if you're going to be backpacker traveling, which will most likely entail carrying your stuff around on your own a lot, going up and down stairs as you check out hotels and hostels, walking through towns sometimes to save on paying for a taxi, hiking to a beach to camp, etc., then you'll want a **backpack** of some sort. If you're planning to bring a **tent** and other **camping items** so that you can camp, then you'll need a full-sized backpack.

Otherwise, you'll probably want to bring a **medium-sized backpack**, because it's imperative to force yourself to bring as little stuff as you can manage, since you will likely be carrying all this stuff around on your back, having to stuff it into the overhead bins on trains and buses, or deal with it sitting on your lap, etc.

The best idea is to go down to your local outdoors store and talk with them about the different types of backpacks, so that they can help you out individually based on your own specific needs. It will depend a lot on whether you're going to bike around the Greek isles, backpack around Europe, hang out on the beaches of Thailand, go trekking in Nepal, etc. For different types of trips you will likely want a different kind of bag or backpack based on the different items you will need to bring along.

And if you're just going to Phuket, Thailand for a week, or to Paris or Santorini, Greece, or to California where you'll be renting a car and then driving around, perhaps you'll just bring the age-old **suitcase**, which will of course look a little more presentable if you'll be staying mostly in decent hotels. So it's up to you as to what works best for your type of trip. As mentioned previously, there is a wide range of ways to travel that can be considered budget travel.

Now, it's what goes *in* the backpack or suitcase or other carrying bag that will really make a difference in your traveling experience. And many of these items are universally useful regardless of what sort of trip you will be taking; whereas others are, of course, specific to certain types of trips.

The first is some sort of a **day pack**—something that you can use while walking around during the day, when most of your stuff is back in your hotel room and you won't want to use your main travel bag to haul around a few essential items, such as water, rain jacket, food, camera, etc. The other advantage to a day pack of some sort is that it gives you some more places to put things, especially if you get one with lots of little pockets. So it won't be just taking up space in your bag while you're getting from Point A to Point B, but will actually make use of itself by being somewhere to put an assortment of different items. This, however, might be something that you'll want to wait until you arrive at your destination country to buy. In cheaper countries in Asia, for example, you can buy great little bags that are a fraction of the cost for something similar in the West, are colorful, blend in a little better with the local style, and make a great souvenir to bring back home. One way or another though, you'll want to have something to carry things around with you while you're sightseeing and exploring.

Needles, thread, and **compact scissors** can come in extremely handy for a variety of unexpected circumstances. Perhaps a strap on your backpack breaks and you need a quick fix, a shoelace breaks, you get a tear in your new shirt, your shorts start shredding but you're still attached to using them, etc. Toss these small items into a little bag somewhere, and though you won't use them regularly, if you do need them you'll be glad you packed them.

Sleeping bag or blanket—many budget hotels, especially in developing countries, as well as hostels, bamboo huts on the beach, etc. will provide a sheet (hopefully cleaned recently!) and pillow, but won't necessarily provide a blanket. I'm guessing it's a combination of saving on having to clean them, as well as not having to worry about replacing them if they're stolen. If you're staying in nicer or even standard hotels, then this is irrelevant. But if you're heading off on a backpacking trip around Asia or many other parts of the world, then you'll need your own sleeping bag or blanket.

This also might be something you want to buy once you get there, particularly if you're going somewhere warm and just need a thin blanket or sheet of some kind. You might want to wait to buy something colorful and exotic to carry around with you, rather than just a white sheet or boring blanket. If you're attached to your awesome sleeping bag, however, you'll probably want to bring that.

Just keep in mind where you're going. If you're headed to the beaches of Greece or Thailand, anywhere in the tropics really, Africa, etc. (in other words, anywhere it's going to be hot), you don't want to be sweating away in your sleeping bag that's designed for keeping you warm in the Rocky Mountains. Buy another, thinner sleeping bag, which will also take up less space and be lighter to carry around; or else some sort of a thin blanket that will pack small.

Clothing is of course pretty self-explanatory. If you're headed to Iceland in the winter, you'll probably want to pack the long underwear! And if you're headed to Indonesia, you'll want shorts, tank tops and a rain jacket. This is where the *"when in doubt, leave it out"* rule applies the most. Unless you're going trekking in Nepal and need special trekking clothing, or doing something else with a specific focus, clothing can be bought anywhere and you don't want to be carrying around stuff that you don't need. I would recommend bringing plenty of **underwear**, and **t-shirts**. Underwear is something that most of us are a tad picky about, and generally the longer you can extend the underwear, the longer you can put off doing laundry. And t-shirts are something small and light, that alone can make you feel as if you've got a wide array of outfits to choose from.

Pants, especially jeans are fun to shop for in other parts of the world. I have loads of cool jeans that I've bought in various places, for just a few dollars and in styles I wouldn't have found back home in the U.S. And **shorts** are easy to come by, as are new **sandals, jackets**, pretty much everything else you might need clothing-wise. So, if you're pondering whether you need two pairs of pants or one, whether you should bring sandals and **shoes** (which I never bring to Asia, other than when exploring the mountains, and which I buy when I get there), or else just the sandals, etc., there's really no reason to take more stuff. Shopping in foreign countries is one of the funnest things you'll do. Leave it out...and if it turns out you needed it—they wear shoes in other parts of the world, too!

Most of the rest of the items on my list are pretty self-explanatory. One that I will elaborate on is the **small key/combination locks**. In India and in other parts of the developing world, many of the budget hotels (often the same sorts of places that might not provide blankets) don't actually provide locks for their room doors, so you will need your own. (In that case there will be a sturdy latch that you will use to lock the door using your own lock.) I actually prefer this, because it means that you, and you alone can get into your room. So it leaves less reason to worry while you're away that someone from the hotel with a second key might be going through your stuff.

Also, it's good to have a few of these small locks for staying in hostels, so that you can lock your backpack up while you're gone for the day, i.e. along with a **thin metal cord that loops through your backpack**, and then around a bed post or something else that isn't going anywhere. And if you'll be camping, you can lock your tent for some minimal extra protection against someone popping into your tent and grabbing things. And this can also come in handy for locking your backpack up while sleeping overnight on a train. So those are some other small, yet useful items that you might as well throw into the bottom of a bag somewhere, and which may come in very handy.

Grapefruit seed extract and a **water purifier** such as **chlorine dioxide** are definitely optional, and you probably won't need them. But they're two things I always throw into the bag, just in case. Grapefruit seed extract is supposed to be extremely effective against stomach parasites, in case you should get a case of the **"Delhi belly"** as the say, or something worse such as **giardia**. I talked to someone first-hand who said that after years of dealing with giardia, it was what finally cured it for him. And chlorine dioxide or some other type of water purifier such as **iodine**, or a **water filter** is something you would definitely need when camping and drinking water out of streams and lakes...but won't necessarily need traveling. However, it's also something you won't have an easy time finding in a foreign country. So I bring it just in case I might end up in a situation where I need to drink water that could be questionable—such as if I were to spontaneously go camping somewhere, i.e. on a secluded beach where there happened to be a stream nearby.

With all that said, I have one final word of advice regarding packing: *spread everything you're planning to take with you out on the floor.* Now, go through every item you have there, little and big, take a good hard look at it and decide whether you really need it and/or whether it's actually going to enhance your traveling experience. For example, you may be going to tropical paradise, but are you *actually* going to end up using a **hammock** very often?? Maybe so! But maybe not. Or else maybe you'll get there, there are hammocks galore already, and you now have to haul around your fancy new hammock for the rest of your trip without making good use of it. And if you're planning to go snorkeling at some point on your trip, but won't be at the beach every day, how about just bringing some **swim goggles**, instead of a **snorkel, mask and fins**? Swim goggles take up almost zero room. And with a decent pair you can see things underwater with them almost as good as you can with an actual snorkeling mask.

And how about the **hair dryer**, the large bottle of your favorite **shampoo**, your favorite **pillow** or **stuffed animal**, several large **books** you may or may not actually read, etc. I'm not saying not to bring these items. But how about pouring some of your favorite shampoo into a much smaller bottle? And maybe this is the time to take a break from blow-drying; perhaps even from your stuffed animal, too? And yes, they do have pillows over there! And how about just bringing one good book, and then trade them in for others along the way? (There are used bookstores in many countries where you can sell your books. And many hostels and guest houses have a "library" shelf, in which you can exchange one book for another one.) The point is, keep in mind that you're going to be dealing with this stuff almost every day, for weeks or months. A lighter pack makes a huge difference when it comes to getting from Point A to Point B, which you'll be doing a lot of.

You don't want to be walking across a hot, noisy city; or perhaps hiking to an awesome beach that someone told you about, where you'll sleep under the stars...while sweating away in the hot sun as you're cursing yourself for bringing along a **tennis racket** you thought you'd make use of at some point, or a **guitar**, or your favorite heavy book of quotations, or a wooden **chess set**, or who knows what else...Then again, maybe it will be worth it once you get there, and you can then play chess and guitar and tennis on the beach. But better to think hard about it *now, before* you get on the plane; rather than have to deal with these bulky items later on, that you've realized you don't really need in a foreign country.

Chapter 9—*Carry-on items when flying*

One thing I've forgotten more than once in the packing process, is to keep in mind the fact that certain items can't be taken onto the plane as carry-on items. We all know pretty well by now that knives, scissors, liquids and other items aren't allowed with us on the plane; but sometime it's easy to forget, amidst all the other preparations, that we have to factor this in.

The thing to do is the night before your flight, as you're doing the final packing—get your carry-on bag ready to go with the things you will want for the flight, **keeping in mind to put the things that**

aren't allowed into your checked bag (your big backpack or suitcase). This may be obvious, but it's always worth a second reminder. Here's where bringing a day pack with you comes in handy right away, because that's your carry-on bag. Now, don't pack the way that you're going to want things to be when you arrive. You'll have to reshuffle once you've gotten to wherever you're going; but that's just the way it goes.

So pack your day pack or other carry-on bag FIRST. Look through everything you're bringing on your trip, and sort out what you'll want with you on the plane: your book, an extra shirt that can act as a pillow or blanket, snacks, water bottle (WITHOUT water in it, since liquids aren't allowed), your passport, moneybelt or wallet with ID, traveler's checks, credit cards, your earplugs and sleeping mask, journal and pen, cell phone, laptop, etc.

Side note: By the way, do you have some currency for the country that you're flying into? This isn't necessarily needed, but it's worth mentioning (and thinking about *before* you get to your final packing). In particular if you'll be arriving in the evening or the middle of the night, it's probably a good idea to find out if moneychangers will be open at the time that you arrive. You don't want to get there and find yourself stuck with no cash on hand to catch a taxi to your hotel. However, this most likely will not be a problem, in particular if you have an ATM card as one of your ways of accessing your cash, since they will be open 24 hours.

But if you will be relying on moneychangers to change currency or else cash traveler's checks, here's a story of my own that will illustrate something to keep in mind:

Once when I was flying to **Bangkok, Thailand**, I had a layover in **Taipei, Taiwan**. I didn't have any **Thai baht** (the Thailand currency) on me, as I was assuming the moneychangers would still be open, even though I was flying in at around 11pm. I was surprised however to discover that the moneychanging desk in the Taipei airport had closed at 3:50pm! No, not 3pm, 3:30 or 4, but precisely at 3:50. Strange. But anyway, this got me wondering if the moneychangers in the Bangkok airport would then be open when I arrived after 11pm.

It occurred to me to make use of the Lonely Planet forum. I didn't have a laptop at the time; but I found a computer in the airport where I could access the internet, and posted a thread in the Thailand section explaining my situation, and asking if anyone knew if things would be open later in Bangkok than they were in Taipei. I had a couple of hours to kill, so I went off and read a book and then just wandered around a bit; and then came back and checked for some answers a few hours later. Sure enough, I had several replies, all assuring me that in the Bangkok airport, everything was open 24 hours.

So, that's just something to keep in mind before flying: you might want some of the local currency on hand just to be on the safe side (in which case you will need to find a currency conversion office in your local town; which might possibly be your own bank, depending on the type of currency). However, if you do convert some of your cash into the foreign currency of the country you're flying into, **don't convert too much**. Because you will get a better conversion rate inside the country itself, even though the airports don't tend to have the best rates. But it will still be better than somewhere outside the country. *One of the best places to get a good rate is actually through an ATM, because they are obligated to use the current going conversion rate.*

Alright, back to getting packed. So, you'll want to pack up your day pack or other carry-on item as if you're about to walk on the plane with it (which, of course, you will soon be doing), rather than remembering at the last minute and having to rearrange everything in the airport. In particular, take note of the banned items and make sure they are in your checked bag, not in your carry-on: knives, scissors, lighters & matches (although one common lighter and one book of safety matches ARE allowed in your carry on), liquids, gels (including lotions and shampoo), etc. Here's a website with much more information about banned items, either banned completely or simply banned as carry-ons, but allowed in your checked baggage:

http://www.airsafe.com/danger.htm

In short, just keep it in mind well before you check in to separate your stuff appropriately...so that you don't find yourself sweating in the security line, wondering if you're going to end giving up a personal possession, because your checked bag is already on its way to the plane.

Chapter 10—*Travel insurance*

Whether or not you choose to buy travel insurance is of course up to you. Keep in mind that in a select few countries, for example the **Czech Republic**, proof of health insurance is actually required in order to enter the country. You also may be required to have health or travel insurance if going on a cruise, or participating in an organized tour. However, for the most part it isn't required. I didn't buy travel insurance for my first several trips, simply because I always assumed it would be outrageously expensive. Fortunately, it doesn't have to be. The insurance I've gotten for my last several trips is about $1.60 per day. Since I'm not an expert on the ins and outs, pluses and minuses of various insurance policies, I'll simply recommend the company that I always go with, which is World Nomads (**http://www.worldnomads.com**). They cater to budget travelers, and cover a wide variety of adventurous activities, such as trekking. And they seem like a very reputable company. So feel free to do your own research and make your own decision. But that at least gives you one option to consider and look further into.

Part 2: Favorite Places in the World

In this section I will list and briefly describe some of my favorite places that I've visited in the course of my travels. ***Note that this isn't meant to be a substitute for a guidebook.*** I won't go in-depth with things such as bus or train times, specific hotels and restaurants (unless one was particularly noteworthy), prices of attractions, etc.

Instead, this part is simply meant to highlight and briefly review some places to consider for your next adventure, including many places that you may not have heard much about (or else give my own perspective on a few of the more popular places). I will focus more on my favorite spots than necessarily the most well-known, and only review those I've actually visited in person. However, virtually all of the places I will cover here will also be covered to some extent in the budget guidebooks (depending on which one you have), so that you can find out some more specific information about the place if needed.

Chapter 11—*India*

First, a few general thoughts about **India**. India is truly the land of extremes. If you go there, you will likely find it to be one of the most rewarding places you will ever travel to, as well as one of the most challenging. And depending on where you end up, you may experience more of the challenging aspects of this very different part of the world, rather than the rewards.

My best advice regarding India is to avoid the big cities as much as possible; unless you happen to enjoy congestion, garbage, pollution, crowds, noise, hawkers, hustlers, scams, more expensive lodging, etc. Although the **Taj Mahal** is certainly a must-see, and it's always a part of getting to know a country to experience its capital city or other major metropolitan areas, the downsides far outweigh the upsides in my opinion. Sure, go to the Taj Mahal, spend a day or two in **Delhi** or **Mumbai.** But I highly recommend not planning your trip to India around hopping from one big city to another. The best places in India, in my own subjective opinion, are the small towns and villages and out-of-the-way spots, many of which I will detail below. And even when it comes to interesting attractions, most of the best ones aren't located in the big cities.

Virtually all of the places that I will mention here, with perhaps one or two exceptions depending on which guidebook you use, are covered to some extent in the guidebooks (at least those that cater to more adventurous travelers, such as the **Lonely Planet** and **Rough**

Guide). So if a place I mention sounds particularly intriguing, I would suggest then looking it up in a guidebook once you have one, to get another perspective on it, as well as find some more specific information about it. Also you might try visiting the Lonely Planet online forum, plug it into the search engine and see what further info you come across from those other travelers who have visited there in person.

The "Golden Triangle"—Delhi, Agra and Jaipur:

Very quickly, I will give my opinion on the "Golden Triangle", which is the most popular tourist route in India, in particular for those who are only visiting for a week or less. It incorporates the cities of **Delhi**, **Agra** (where the **Taj Mahal** is located), and the city of **Jaipur**.

In short, these three cities are some of my least favorite places in India! However, there are also still reasons to visit all three. Delhi is often the cheapest place to fly into and out of, and I've flown there on 3 out of 4 of my trips to India. There are still things to see, there's certainly plenty of excitement, and it of course offers one view of life in India. In particular, I would say that the new, very impressive **Akshardham Temple** is worth a visit (it can be easily reached on the subway system as it's near a subway stop of the same name); as well as **Humayun's Tomb**. The **Red Fort** pales in comparison to other forts around India, with the view from outside being the most impressive sight of it, so you might want to save your money rather than pay to enter. However the nearby **Grand Mosque (Jama Masjid)**is incredible and definitely a must-see. And exploring the winding maze of alleys of **Old Delhi** around the Grand Mosque is guaranteed to be an interesting experience.

In **Agra**, it's all about the **Taj Mahal**, which is absolutely exquisite, one-of-a-kind and holds its place as one of the most beautiful buildings in the world quite easily. There are many budget hotels and guest houses in the "**Taj Ganj**" area right nearby. Stay for a day or two to see the Taj Mahal, and then move on from this dirty, congested, polluted city.

Jaipur tops the list of my least favorite city in India (at least, of those I spent any time in). However I only visited it for a few days in 1999, so perhaps things have changed since then! (Probably not.) However the nearby **Amber Fort** is truly amazing and very much worth a visit. It was the only monument I visited in or near Jaipur, so perhaps there are other things worth seeing (I'm sure there are many). But overall I would say don't waste your precious time in another dirty, congested, chaotic city filled with gem sellers hassling you at every street corner. Instead, move on to some of the much more pleasant places to spend your time in India, mostly smaller towns and villages.

Pushkar:

Nearby to Jaipur is the mystical and very interesting little village of **Pushkar**, site of the largest camel fair in India which takes place every November. Pushkar is also one of the most touristy places in India when it comes to Western backpackers. But, that's part of the fun. It's a great place to meet people, watch the colorful, characterful Indian **sadhus** (wandering holy mean)and **gypsies** wandering about, hang out for the day sipping smoothies and trying the wide variety of dishes from around the world at the many restaurants catering to the international travelers. Just watch out for the wily gypsy women, who will insist on giving you a "free" henna tattoo, only to then ask for an exorbitant fee afterwards!

There are loads of temples within the village; and also two temples situated on nearby hills that are both fun hikes and give astounding 360-degree views of the surrounding countryside. You can take a camel ride into the surrounding desert, or simply go for a wander and see who and what you come across. You can also organize a multi-day camel trek; however I would suggest going further west to **Jaiselmer**, or even better to **Kuri**, both of which I talk about further below. Pushkar is also great for shopping, and for accessing the Internet, with tons of Internet cafes. When I was last there in 2008, it was ten rupees (25 cents) per hour! In short, Pushkar is one of those places where you get a taste of the peaceful, spiritual side of India, with plenty of conveniences. Perhaps not exactly "real India", but still undoubtedly a fun place to hang out on your way to and from other destinations.

Almora:

Almora is a pleasant little town in the foothills of the **Himalaya Mountains** of northern India, in the little-visited **Kumaon** region of eastern **Uttarakhand State**, situated along the western border of **Nepal**. Almora is situated atop a ridge that looks out over a wide valley, with spectacular views of some of the highest peaks of the Himalaya Mountains stretched out within clear view. Near Almora is an area known as **Kasar Devi**, which is where many of the foreign travelers stay, in one of the many guesthouses that line a ridge jutting out with great views of the snowy peaks from various angles. I visited there in the early winter months, when it was warm during the day, but quite cold at night. Keep in mind that Indian budget hotels and guest houses don't usually provide heating! So come prepared for the cold evenings with long underwear, warm socks, hat, jacket, etc., because the evening will likely be spent either walking around in the cold night air to keep warm, or else huddled in your room!

Joshimath:

Whereas in Almora I was looking out at the Himalaya Mountains off in the distance, **Joshimath** is smack IN the Himalaya—the same white snowy peaks I was seeing from afar at Almora. It's a long ways up there, but seriously worth it. Joshimath is the nearest town to the **Badrinath temple**, which is a major destination for Hindu pilgrims. However, because I was there in early winter, the temple was closed. I was lucky. The winter snows hadn't arrived yet, the days were warm and I was able to walk around in a t-shirt at times. Evening and nights, however were definitely cold. There's a lot to see in the area. You can hike up to the ski resort that rests on top of the mountain high above the town; or explore a couple of different roads out of town that get you different views of the mountains. Shared jeep taxis (or else your own private one) are the best way to get out of town; or else just start walking, and you can always flag one down on your way back to town.

Rishikesh:

Rishikesh is one of the most popular destinations in India for budget travelers, in part because it's known as the **"Yoga capital of the world"**, and many Westerners go there to practice yoga, meditation and other spiritual endeavors. Rishikesh is also where **The Beatles** visited in the 1960s and studied meditation with **Maharishi Mahesh Yogi**. Despite the fact that it's so touristy and well-known, it's still one of my favorite places in India. For one thing, it's a good place to start your trip to India, especially if you're flying into Delhi, as it's relatively close, about 5 hours north by train. Situated on the **Ganges River** where the river is just flowing out of the Himalaya mountain foothills, it's in a spectacular location of scenic natural beauty.

Keep in mind that the main area where travelers stay isn't actually in the town of Rishikesh itself, which is really just another bustling Indian town, of little interest to travelers other than a good place to do some shopping. Instead, you will want to catch a taxi, rickshaw, or just walk north about 2 kilometers, to a footbridge called the **Ram Jhula**, that goes over the Ganges River to a quiet and very atmospheric area (known as **Swarg Ashram**) of ashrams, restaurants, guest houses and tourist shops lined along the Ganges. Basically, you can stay there as long as you like and have everything you need. There's also plenty to do from walking around and taking in the sights of **Hindu pilgrims** bathing in the river, cows and monkeys scattered about, spiritual **"sadhus"** (wandering homeless men committed to the spiritual path), enjoy the music and incense wafting through the air, take a pick of the many restaurants, etc. There are even nice sandy beaches along the Ganges (which you can swim in here as the water is clean, since there are no cities further upstream), as well as good out-of-the-way spots to read a book, meditate, practice yoga or just sit and watch the river flow by.

Mussoorie:

Mussoorie is an Indian **"hill station"**, which are towns set up by the **British** all over India in the mountains as places to get away from the suffocating Indian heat during the summers. Mussoorie is now a very popular tourist destination for Indians. It is by no means unknown to foreign tourists, but doesn't seem to be a popular stop for foreigners. I had no expectations when going there, but was pleasantly surprised. It's an interesting, clean and colorful little town scattered along a narrow ridge. If you walk up to the north-facing hills, you'll get some great views of the Himalaya. I visited there in January, when it was cool during the day and quite cold at night. The advantage was, it wasn't very busy. I would guess that during the summer it could turn into quite a zoo.

Keechen:

Wow, **Keechen**! One of the most amazing experiences of India, unexpectedly so. It's not even in the Lonely Planet book, and was given just a paragraph in the Rough Guide. I visited there because it was a convenient halfway stop between **Bikaner** and **Jaiselmer**, so I decided to stay for the night. Keechen is the site of a tiny village, and where **Demoiselle cranes** have been fed for more than a hundred years, every morning and evening. They know to arrive at the time of dawn and dusk, when they swirl in from the sky by the hundreds all at the same time. Also, the village there is quite interesting. It seems to be about 70% abandoned, as many of the buildings are falling apart. And there are many more varieties of birds by a lake nearby that is an unofficial bird sanctuary. If you're headed out to Jaiselmer, and want somewhere interesting and unique to stop for the night, I highly recommend it. To get there, you will need to go through the nearby larger town of **Phalodi**, and then catch an auto rickshaw to Keechen. I wish I had video to share of those cranes flying in to feed, but this was before I had a digital camera. I guess you'll just have to go there and see it for yourself!

Jaiselmer:

Jaiselmer is another super popular place that's still very much worth visiting. It's out of the way in the far western part of **Rajasthan** state, but it's worth making the trip out there. Situated in the **Thar desert**, the town and its spectacular fort rises out of the desert on a hill with amazing views in every direction. Most of the town is carved out of sandstone, and many of the buildings are exquisitely constructed, so that just walking around the town and exploring its winding maze of cobble-stoned paths and alleyways is a fascinating way to spend the day. There's also plenty to do and see outside of the town, most notably including camel treks into the desert, which can most likely be arranged through your hotel, or else at any of the many tourist offices in the touristy part of town. It's also a great place for bike rides out of town, with lots of potential destinations including beautiful ancient temples, and smaller villages that make a fun day's adventure getting there and back.

Kuri:

Kuri is just an hour's bus ride outside of Jaiselmer. It is by no means undiscovered; but at least when I visited in 2008, it was fairly untouched. There were several guest houses, but no restaurants, shops or anything else catering to tourists. Meals were prepared by the guest house owners and eaten there. Kuri is in a beautiful region of the Thar desert, and you can see one of the amazing sandy dunes right near the small village, about a 30-minute walk away. Kuri is also a great place to begin a camel trek. I did my camel trek starting at Jaiselmer, but after visiting Kuri, I wished that I had done it starting from there. Kuri is a very peaceful place to spend several days or longer just enjoying the peace and quiet and the authentic Indian village, without the hustle and bustle of more touristy spots.

Orchha:

Orchha has, for unexplained reasons, remained more or less off the tourist map. It is by no means a secret. There's an assortment of guest houses, hotels and restaurants there. However, considering what it has to offer and how close it is to the tourist frenzy in nearby places such as **Agra** and **Khajuraho**, it's amazing that it hasn't become overrun. Orchha is a very small, peaceful and relaxed little village, that is also jam-packed with temples, forts and palaces as it was the seat of a kingdom founded in the 16th century. Legend goes that the first king of the dynasty, **Rudra Pratap Singh**, died trying to save a cow from an attacking lion. There is much to see there, both within the official tourist sites which require a ticket, as well as lots of exploring that you can do on your own, within the ancient ruins in town area as well as in the countryside nearby. I highly recommend renting a bicycle or motor scooter and venturing off on your own to see what you might find.

Mandu:

Mandu is an area of **Muslim ruins** scattered around a wide area. It's difficult to get to, but it's worth it, because of the amazing array of impressive ancient sites there, the gorgeous landscapes (including a canyon that almost rivals the **Grand Canyon** of the United States), plus the fact that there are so few other tourists there...because it's hard to get to! You could spend a good 3-7 days here either doing random exploring, or just enjoying the peace and quiet, reading a good book in your room. Just make sure to get out and watch the incredible sunsets from the **"Sunset view"** looking out over the canyon! The best way to get around is by bicycle, as everything is within biking distance. Or rent a motor scooter if you're feeling lazy. The bus drops you off at the center of "town", if you can call it that. Everything is within a block or so from there...except the ruins, which are scattered over a wider area.

Omkareshwar:

Omkareshwar is so named because it is actually an island in the **Narmada River**, which is apparently shaped like the Indian **"Om" symbol** as seen from above. Due to this, it is considered an extremely spiritual place and is a destination for **Hindu pilgrims**. It is a very mellow little village, and though it is not very popular with foreign tourists, Omkareshwar is completely equipped with everything needed for visitors since it is a popular destination for many Indians. Unfortunately the peaceful ambiance has been marred by a recently constructed dam just upstream from the town area. Although the sight of the dam is a bit of an eyesore, more disturbing than that is the siren that goes off at all hours, to alert residents when the water level is about to change. Still, it's definitely worth stopping for a day or two, particularly if you're on your way to or from some of the other good sites to visit in the area, such as **Mandu** and **Pachmarhi**.

Pachmarhi:

Pachmarhi is another **"hill station"** that was set up by the British as an administrative headquarters for central India during the time the English were occupying India. Pachmarhi is now a popular tourist destination for Indians, but not frequented by many foreign visitors. It is nowhere near anything else that's well-known, which is partly the reason it hasn't caught on with the backpacker travelers (though it is within about a day's travel of Omkareshwar). Pachmarhi is up in elevation a bit from the plains surrounding it, though it is primarily on a plain of its own, surrounded by an assortment of hills and mountains. It's an excellent area for exploring by bicycle or motor scooter, as well as for hiking. There's an amazing variety of different terrain to explore. At times I felt like I was in the African savanna; whereas others I felt like I was hiking in Greece or elsewhere. The town is small but has a large variety of hotels and guesthouses. From there you can just head off in any direction to find something interesting.

Gokarna:

Gokarna is another place that's fairly touristy, but is still very much worth spending a week, or even a month or two! Fifteen years ago or so, it was fairly obscure (I visited first in 1999 and then again in 2011), but now it's firmly on the backpacker's circuit. However, many people still don't know about it simply because it gets eclipsed by the even more popular areas further north in **Goa State.** If you're looking for Arabian beach paradise, with amazing beaches, beautiful sunsets, fellow travelers...but without the pounding techno music, drunken idiots and swarming crowds in nearby Goa, then Gokarna and its nearby beaches is the place: **Kudle Beach, Om Beach** and **Paradise Beach**, all of which can be accessed by a walking path from the village of Gokarna, or else by rickshaw along a road that goes behind the beaches. The bus drops you off near the center of town. If you wish, you can find a place to stay in town. But the better idea is to get yourself out to one of the beaches, where there are plenty of beachside huts or rooms, catering to a wide range of budgets.

Tirupati:

So, have you heard of **Tirupati**? If not, why not? You've heard of **Rome, Italy** and **Mecca, Saudi Arabia**, right? Well, Tirupati surpasses them both as the most popular spiritual pilgrimage destination in the world. Don't worry, even many seasoned India travelers haven't heard of it! Located in the state of **Andhra Pradesh** in southeastern India, Tirupati is a good place to stop on your way from **Chennai** to **Hyderabad** or vice versa. It's an interesting place to get a real taste of India, with the usual busy city streets, pollution and sprawling slums, but not quite as intense as larger cities such as Delhi or Mumbai. The main thing to do here is the pilgrimage walk that goes 20 kms (12 miles) between the city of Tirupati and nearby **Tirumala**. Stay in the city of Tirupati for two nights, and then you can do the walk during your day free. Just be prepared for plenty of staring, because not many Western travelers make it through here.

Rameswaram:

Rameswaram is actually on an island that's just off the coast of southern India, across from **Sri Lanka**; however you can still get there by train as the train goes over a bridge that connects the island with the mainland. Rameswaram is one of the holiest towns in India, and an important pilgrimage destination for Hindus. It's a mellow, peaceful little village by the sea and a major spiritual destination, so there are spiritual **"sadhus"** in abundance. It's a good place to just walk around, take in the mystical vibe and the sights, and see what you come across or who you might end up talking with. It has an authentic spiritual vibe since it's out of the way, little visited by foreign tourists and such a holy town to Hindus.

Chapter 12—*Greece and the Greek isles*

I visited **Greece** twice, once for a month during my trip to Europe in June of 1990; and again for three months in the summer and fall of 2009 (as part of a trip that also included **Egypt** and **Turkey**, both of which I'll review below). I brought a mountain bike with me, and spent most of my time there exploring the islands by bicycle; which is a great way to go, and also an excellent way to bring down your budget as you save tremendously on transportation costs not needing to hire taxis, catch buses or rent a vehicle. And most of the islands are small enough that can do a great deal of exploring by bicycle. Just be prepared for a few hills!

I started off camping. The first island I went to, **Anafi**, I camped for free on a beach, along with a few other travelers who were camping there as well. Next, on the islands of **Naxos** and **Syros**, I camped at official campgrounds. Shortly thereafter, I went back to the mainland for a couple of weeks, where I happened to meet a Greek woman from Athens. She had some free time, and so we ended up traveling together for most of the next three months, including joining me to **Turkey**. We camped for free for a week on the island of **Nisyros;** but other than that mostly stayed in rooms, since split between the two of us it wasn't much more expensive, especially since by this time it was going into off-season. This is a real tip when it comes to traveling in Greece, because there's such a stark contrast between high season and off-season (as opposed to low season during the winter, when virtually nothing would be open as far as tourist amenities). High season is basically from mid-June to early September. During the months of May, early June, late September and October, you will find far less crowds, cooler temperatures (but it's still nice and warm), and the prices of rooms will come down considerably.

Athens and the mainland:

Athens is by no means an exceptionally beautiful city. But it is still an interesting place that's worth a few days of your trip, depending on how much time you have. If you're only on a week's vacation to the islands, I would say consider skipping it altogether, if you find a flight direct onto one of the islands. Or else simply plan to spend a day there to see the **Parthenon** & the **Acropolis** (which the Parthenon sits atop) and some of the other ancient sites in that area; as well as **Syntagma Square** and the shopping districts nearby. If you're visiting Greece on a more extended trip, then you might want to stay in Athens for a few days to do a little more in-depth exploring. The Parthenon is undoubtedly a must-see; but other than that I would say your time will be better spent elsewhere in Greece.

I will mostly focus on the Greek islands, but there is certainly much to see on the mainland. The ruins at **Delphi** are spectacular, and the landscapes in that region are also astounding; it's well worth a visit. The **Peloponnese** region is all-around fun and interesting to explore with many sleepy little villages and an assortment of ancient sites, including castles used during the **Crusades**. In particular I can recommend the town of **Leonidio**, on the eastern-central side of the Peloponnese; as well as the inland village of **Kastanitsa** for something completely different, a heavily forested region with amazing mountain views.

I highly recommend the trek up **Mt. Olympus**. I did it in 1990 when I was 18. You don't need a guide, just some basic hiking smarts and some legs that are in the mood for a lot of uphill climbing. The trailhead starts in the village of **Pironia**, where you can find somewhere to leave a few of your things that you don't want to hike up to the top of the mountain (I left my big backpack in the hostel where I stayed, and then just took my day pack). From there you can do the trek in two days, staying the night (and eating meals) at a hostel partway up the mountain called **"Refuge A"**.

I also highly recommend visiting the amazing Eastern Orthodox monasteries at **Meteora** (a UNESCO World Heritage Site), in north-central Greece, which are perched at the tops of stunning sandstone rock pillars. The landscapes of that region are also out-of-this-world mind-blowing.

Lastly, I'll recommend the **Pelion Peninsula**, a few hours drive north of Athens. The nearest large city is **Volos**. The region is little-visited by foreign tourists, despite the fact that it's stunningly beautiful and, in comparison to many other parts of Greece, is very green and lush. Also, there's a beautiful beach there where they filmed one of the scenes from the movie **Mama Mia!** This is a great area to just rent a car, or hop on a bicycle (if you don't mind some hills!) and do some aimless exploring to see what you come across, because there are no large cities there to get lost in, and the entire area is gorgeous, peaceful and very mystical.

Now, on to the islands!

Santorini:

Anyone who knows anything about Greece in the slightest (as well as many who don't) has heard of **Santorini**, as it's one of the most popular Greek isles and famous for one of the most iconic and photographed Greek images, the white houses with blue trim, set against the deep blue waters of the **Mediterranean** and the blue sky.

So the question is, does the reality match up with the hype?? My own answer is a resounding "Yes!" Despite the fact that it's super touristy and no doubt has lost a lot of its authentic charm as a result, it's still a stunningly beautiful place, with a lot to offer. The views looking out over the Mediterranean Sea and the volcanic crater are unparalleled; the towns are exquisite, in particular **Ia** (where many of the images of the blue and white homes are taken, as well as spectacular sunset pictures). It has great beaches and ancient ruins. So, what's not to like?

Now, I must qualify my own personal experience there, by mentioning that I visited there twice, once in June of 1990, before peak tourist season; and again in October of 2009, well after peak tourist season. So, I haven't experienced it with the full force of the teeming tourist crowds. This was somewhere that being there in off-season really paid, literally. When I visited in October of 2009 (with my Greek girlfriend), we paid just 30 Euro for a very nice room that would have been 2-3 times as much as that during peak season.

Rhodes:

Rhodes is another one of the most popular of the Greek isles. However, my review of Rhodes will be markedly different from that of Santorini. In short, of the thirteen Greek isles I visited during my two trips to Greece, it was easily my least favorite. The main city, **Rhodes City**, is overly-touristy. And besides, who wants to go to the Greek

Isles to hang out in the city? Not me, anyway. The Greek isles are all about sleepy little villages, peace, quiet, tranquillity and minimal hassle. Although the old town area of Rhodes City is certainly interesting, it was jam-packed with tourists and there was constant hassle from hustlers trying to get you into their shops and restaurants.

Elsewhere on the island, I was similarly unimpressed (though we didn't drive to the more southerly parts of the island). Things just felt kind of ragged and run-down. The beaches were of the wide, long variety with a road behind them, rather than cozier little private coves, and the sea was a bit rough making it difficult to swim.

Now, that's not to say that there's nothing to see there. We did a drive up and over the center of the island through alpine forest that was beautiful. And we only spent a few days there, so I'm sure that I missed some worthwhile things to see. But, with so many beautiful, peaceful Greek islands that do a much better job of matching what you might expect, I wouldn't recommend going to Rhodes at all, unless you have lots of time on the islands, and it happens to be a convenient place to stop for a day or two while transiting to another island.

Anafi:

Anafi, the next island on the ferry line just past Santorini, isn't the place to go if you're looking for night life, excitement, great shopping, etc. There's just one very small village on the island. However, it *is* a great place to go if you're looking for peace and quiet on the beach, and enjoy hiking around on your own and assorted random exploring. There are some great, secluded beaches, which you can camp on (I did so for a week). The island is popular with young Greeks, and many of the beaches are nude beaches. The town, situated on top of a ridge, is beautiful, with amazing views looking out over the Mediterranean, and there are some excellent restaurants. There's even a bus that will take you along the main road and drop you off near some of the beaches. Or bring your own bike (as I did) to get around. Just be prepared for some major hills! Anafi might not be the best choice for a family vacation. But if you're adventurous, don't have high expectations in the luxury department, and are looking for something different that's off the main tourist trail, then Anafi is a great choice.

Milos:

Milos is an excellent all-around island with a lot to see and do, that really has something for everyone. There are clubs and higher-end hotels and restaurants in and around the main town of **Adamas**, which is a pretty little town that's great for taking a stroll along the waterfront, or visiting churches or several museums. There are several other towns to explore; as well as ancient sites including ancient catacombs and a theater. Milos has more beautiful beaches than you will know what to do with, and very unique, strange yet beautiful landscapes that defy description. Many of them require some exploring to find them, preferably by rental car, or else motor scooter. You could certainly still see a lot by bicycle, though it would requite a lot of biking to see the sights that are further away. You really can't go wrong in visiting Milos.

Patmos:

Patmos was definitely one of my favorite Greek isles. It is most famous for being where **St. John** wrote the **Book of Revelation** from the **Bible**, and you can actually visit the cave where he supposedly lived and wrote. However, there are plenty of other reasons to go to Patmos as well. The main port town of **Skala** is a beautiful village scattered around a pretty little bay. Hovering high above is the very sleepy town of **Hora**, with both a castle dedicated to St. John that you can visit, as well as the quintessential maze of quiet, narrow streets, which you can easily get lost in and where you will see more cats than people. And, Patmos has an amazing assortment of beautiful beaches, most of which have very few people on them. The island isn't tiny, but is still small enough that you can explore by bicycle, or else by motor scooter if you're not up for that much effort. I didn't find a beach that was particularly suitable for camping on for free; however there is a campground on the island that's located right on a nice beach.

Lipsi:

Lipsi is a teeny, tiny island not far from Patmos. There isn't a whole lot to do there, but it's certainly worth stopping to investigate for a few days en route to other islands. There's one very pleasant little village at the port with everything you need as far as rooms, restaurants, markets, etc. The beaches there aren't amazing, but will do the trick. One good reason to go to Lipsi is to explore some of the other nearby islands, though we didn't end up doing that. I wouldn't go well out of your way to visit Lipsi, but it still warrants a visit as yet another unique Greek island with its own individual charm and atmosphere.

Leros:

I found **Leros** interesting and worth a visit, without being particularly exceptional. The climate was a little different from other Greek islands such as nearby Patmos, in that it felt a little wetter and more tropical with lusher foliage. (Remember, this is in comparison to the extreme dryness of the other islands! Don't think Hawaii.) There's a **castle** to explore with great views overlooking the island and across the Mediterranean. I don't recall finding any noteworthy beaches, which was definitely a downside. But there are lots of little villages to explore, so it's a good place to spend a day or two simply driving around the island seeing whatever you see. Overall however, I wouldn't rate the island as being near the top of any Greek Isles must-see lists.

Nisyros:

Nisyros is undoubtedly a unique island that's well worth a visit. It's most known for having a volcanic crater at the center of the island, that you can go down into, and even stand right near steam vents emitting hot steam! The landscapes there are truly otherworldly, and there are some nice hikes that can be done in the area. The main town of **Mandraki** is quiet and peaceful, and a nice place to hang out at a restaurant sipping wine and looking out at the sea. There's also a **monastery** and **medieval castle** that can be visited.

For those who enjoy camping on the beach, this is the main reason to go there, as there's a gorgeous nude, black sand beach that involves a bit of a hike on the western side of the island, called **Pahia Ammos** beach. It is apparently very popular with young Greeks who come to stay there for weeks at a time throughout the summer. My girlfriend who I was traveling with, from Athens, was the one who told me about it. We visited in early October however, outside of tourist season, and so we had it all to ourselves. You will have to get yourself to the end of the road on the western side of the island, which might be tough without a car since there's very little traffic. Also, there's no water source there, so you have to hike in your own water. The hike is only 20-30 minutes along the coast. Once you get there, there is ample room for camping in the shade under trees.

Naxos:

It would be really hard to be bored on **Naxos**. There are tons of beaches, it's popular with windsurfers and other similar water sports, there's great hiking, ancient ruins, and lots of interesting towns and villages to explore both on the coast and in the interior of the island. It's one of the more popular islands in Greece; and though the most visited areas are certainly busy, there are other places, whether beaches or elsewhere in which you might have a nice stretch of sand, or hiking trail, etc. to yourself.

One of the more interesting things I did there was hike to **Apalirou Castle** in the interior of the island. Finding where to start the hike can be a bit tricky, but we managed to find it okay with a bit of searching. It involves a great hike, amazing views and the scattered remains of an ancient castle. Also, be sure to explore some of the beautiful little villages in the interior of the island, such as **Filoti**. You can easily get around by motor scooter, if you want to save some money, rather than a rental car. Although it's one of the larger Greek Isles, it still isn't really that big. I did some biking along the coast, but getting into the interior by bicycle would be a bit of a challenge, though not impossible.

Aegina:

The island of **Aegina** is barely a stone's throw from Athens, and you can actually see Athens easily from the island. But despite that, it still feels as if you're out on the islands, a ways away from the bustle of the city. The main town, **Aegina Town** is a bit busy and touristy, but not overly so. I wasn't particularly impressed by the beaches on Aegina. However, there are other good reasons to visit, including an assortment of interesting little villages scattered around the island; the **Temple of Aphaea**, dedicated to a Greek goddess; and most notably, the ancient monastic village of **Paleohora**, which is actually one of the most interesting ancient sites I saw in Greece—far more interesting than the Parthenon, or even Delphi, despite being barely mentioned in my guidebook. Scattered over a hill are dozens of small churches where monks lived for hundreds of years. The churches are open to the public, filled with beautiful, colorful frescoes and paintings, and even have candles burning in them despite the fact that there's no admission fee to enter the site and no one seems to be around attending to them. So, despite a lack of great beaches, Aegina has plenty to offer, particularly if you're only in the mood for a one-hour ferry ride from Athens.

Chapter 13—*Turkey*

Turkey is a fascinating country in many ways. It straddles the boundaries, literally and figuratively, between the West and the Middle East. It's **Muslim**, but much more culturally progressive than most Muslim countries. The capital of **Istanbul** feels like an equal mix of the

Middle East and Europe, and is one of my favorite cities of the world. I spent three weeks in Turkey, which wasn't nearly enough time in my book. (I prefer to spend months in a country, but a few weeks is certainly better than nothing!)

Istanbul:

As mentioned above, I really liked **Istanbul**. I had no expectations really because I hadn't done a lot of reading about Turkey before arriving. This was in the midst of my trip to Greece and also Egypt, and so I'd been too busy traveling to do a lot of research. I also visited Turkey with my Greek girlfriend. We stayed at an affordable hostel (which we booked through hostelworld.com) in the most popular tourist area of Istanbul (the "Historical" area of Istanbul) , just a short ways from the famous **Blue Mosque**. This area is great for walking around with a lot to see: great shopping, restaurants, historical sights, etc. You can get around to other parts of Istanbul using the very convenient light rail system. There are several impressive shopping districts around Istanbul, including the **Akmerkez**, which was actually recognized as the best shopping district in the world in 1996! So, plan to spend a few days in Istanbul, or longer, depending on how much time you have allotted for your trip .

Pamukkale:

Pamukkale, a UNESCO World Heritage site, means "cotton castle" in Turkish, and when you see some images of it you'll understand why. It is an amazing area of natural hot springs and other geothermal phenomenon, including a white chalky substance known as **"travertine"** that was created by the flowing hot water that emerges naturally from the ground. The main area to visit is around the area of the natural hot pools, which is also the site of the ancient city of **Hierapolis**. There are many ancient ruins from Hierapolis scattered around the area just above the main area of hot pools, which adds to the ambience and history of the area. Though it's a little out of the way, I would highly recommend visiting Pamukkale on your trip to Turkey if you're planning to be in that part of the country.

Termessos:

Termessos is an amazing site of ancient ruins about 20 miles (30 kilometers) outside of the medium-sized city of **Antalya**. You pretty much need a vehicle to get there, as it's up a road that branches off of the main highway. You'll come to a parking lot at a trailhead, and then it involves a fairly short but steep hike that can be done as a loop in order to see most of the ruins. There's no entry fee, but there are signs giving information about the sites, such as the amazing amphitheatre. The ruins of this ancient city date back to at least the time of **Alexander the Great**. The setting is stunning, with amazing views all the way back to the city of Antalya, out to sea and of the impressive, rocky mountains that the ancient city is situated within. Definitely well worth a visit, especially if you're staying for a night or two in the nearby city of Antalya.

Kabak, Oludeniz and The Lycian Way trek:

I originally intended to visit Turkey with plans to hike the **Lycian Way**, which is a 300-mile (500 kilometer) trek that goes from the tiny village of **Kabak** to the city of **Antalya**, along the south coast of Turkey through a region with few roads. Due to various circumstances—including getting to Turkey later in the season than expected, getting low on money and having spontaneously met up with Dianna who couldn't have done the hike due to a bad knee—those plans got scrapped. I do hope to go back to Turkey again someday in order to complete this amazing hike. There's much more info about the trek at **http://www.lycianway.com**.

This area as a whole however is well worth a visit. The natural beauty is amazingly stunning, and there are great beaches in the area, as well as more ancient ruins. If you enjoy adventurous outdoor activities, this is definitely the place to go. We stayed at Kabak, which is at the end of the road and barely even a village, but I wanted to get a taste at least for the Lycian Way trek. But you could also stay in the more substantial towns of **Fethiye** or **Oludeniz**. We only spent a few days in the area, but it was apparent that you could easily spend a week or more exploring this fascinating region.

Cappadocia:

If there's one place you must visit in Turkey—in fact, if there's one place you must visit in the world—it's **Cappadocia**. I hadn't read much about it until I started looking through my recently purchased guidebook just a few days before flying from Athens to Istanbul; so again I didn't have much expectation. But I was absolutely blown away by the amazingness of it all. We spent five days there, and could have spent longer. You could easily spend a couple of weeks there exploring, without even seeing all of the sites.

Cappadocia is a strange mix of fascinating geological phenomenon, as well as very complex and mysterious human history. All throughout a wide region of hundreds of square miles are strange **"fairy chimneys"** (pillars of rock sticking up out of the ground) and assorted rock formations, that truly defy description and boggle the mind. To describe it as otherworldly is an understatement. And then, on top of that, humans have lived there for thousands of years—no one really knows for exactly how long—and they carved caves into these strange rock formations, making them look even stranger. **Christian monks** also lived in the area, and there are churches carved out of pure rock, covered inside with amazing, brilliantly colorful frescoes depicting the life of Christ.

In addition to all that, going back even further in time, entire cities were constructed completely underground, that could accommodate up to 50,000 people, such as at the site of **Derinkuyu**. It is believed this was done as a result of periods of intense warfare, when people retreated underground as the only option to escape being overrun by their enemies. Nothing of these cities can be seen from above ground. Instead, you go down some stairs (such as at the site of Derinkuyu which can be toured in part, though much of the site is still off limits), that turns into a narrow tunnel which then reveals a maze of more tunnels, rooms, air ventilation shafts, even larger spaces that were apparently churches of some sort, all carved completely out of the rock underground, going down twelve levels. It absolutely staggers the imagination to think about the society that must have existed within such a place, in which the residents must have rarely seen the light of day.

The main tourist hub for Cappadocia is **Goreme**, which is where myself and Dianna stayed, in a guest house that featured rooms that were actually ancient caves, refurbished to include electric lighting, bathroom, carpeting, a comfy bed and everything else a picky tourist might need. And, the views from there looking out at the town of Goreme and the surrounding, surreal landscapes were absolutely astounding. Ideally, you will want to rent a car in order to properly explore Cappadocia, since the sights are spread out over a wide area. However, if you're on a tight budget, then there's plenty to see right in the town of Goreme and within walking distance from there. In fact, the amazing thing about this area is that many of the most fascinating sights aren't marked, don't require an entry fee and have no other people around. You just start hiking off into the countryside, and you'll come across ancient caves, sometimes with colorful Christian murals and frescoes, and the landscapes themselves are beyond anything else you've ever seen.

One of the most popular "official" sights to visit in Cappadocia is the **Goreme Open Air Museum**, which is a UNESCO World Heritage site and features dozens of rock-cut churches carved out by Christian monks, featuring the most amazing Christian frescoes of the region. But keep in mind that right nearby, completely free, are other ancient sites to visit. After visiting the Open Air Museum, we parked our car nearby and went hiking off away from the crowds, where we found sites that were similarly fascinating, yet with none of the tourist crowds. In short, if you get the chance to visit Turkey, make sure to visit Cappadocia, and give yourself ample time to explore. You will not be disappointed, I can guarantee you that!

Chapter 14—*Egypt*

I visited **Egypt** as part of my 4 ½-month trip to Greece, Egypt and Turkey in the fall of 2009. This was just a little over a year before the revolution that completely changed Egypt's political and cultural landscape. Egypt's future is undoubtedly unknown and unpredictable, with the military currently in charge after a revolution demanding real democracy. Elections are apparently scheduled for June of 2012. Before making plans to visit Egypt, it would obviously be advised to look further into the current political situation, since things are changing rapidly and no one knows when further protests, or even violence may break out next.

All that being said, Egypt is an incredible country with some of the most fascinating and ancient known history on the planet. It had always been a dream of mine to visit the **Great Pyramids**, and I consider myself lucky to have had the chance to see them in person, as anyone who has done so will no doubt agree. But there is much more to Egypt than only **Cairo** and the Pyramids. I spent three weeks there in October and November. This was a good time to visit as it was relatively cool, but still plenty warm during the daytime. Yet it wasn't quite peak tourist season, which is around Christmas and New Year's and then through Easter. But anytime from October to May is a good time to go; unless, of course, you happen to prefer the scorching heat of summer.

Cairo and the Great Pyramids:

Cairo is a fascinating city worth several days of exploring. My Lonely Planet guidebook made a rather remarkable statement regarding the city: "there are no bad neighborhoods of Cairo". It advised that you could walk around the city as you pleased, without worrying about crossing into areas that might be hostile to foreigners. And though I certainly didn't traverse the entire city or even a fraction thereof, I found this to be pretty accurate. People were overall incredibly friendly, other than the expected hustlers trying to get you into their shops in the more touristy areas. Even on the subway, the vibe was actually much more friendly and personable than on the New York City subway. Since I haven't been there since the revolution took place, I have no idea how things may have changed in real terms. I would strongly suggest checking the Lonely Planet Thorn Tree forum, or some other traveler's forum along those lines, to get some current information from other travelers who have been there more recently.

The **Great Pyramids of Giza** live up to their illustrious title like few other monuments possibly can. I'll leave the specific information to your Egypt guidebook as far as their history, construction and other details, other than to say that as fascinating as it is to read about the mysterious circumstances involving how they could have possibly been created by humans thousands of years ago, seeing them in person amplifies all those nagging questions immeasurably. The **Giza Complex** or **Giza Necropolis** includes not just the three Great Pyramids of **Khufu**, **Khafre** and **Menkaure**, but also the three **Queens Pyramids**, the **Sphinx**, ancient cemeteries, a workers village, the valley pyramids and more.

I spent about six hours exploring the areas both right near the pyramids and the Sphinx, as well as further away in the desert, from where you can get spectacular views of the pyramids, as well as of the city of Cairo off in the distance, which creates quite the contrast as a backdrop. If you want to get some good photographs, I recommend giving yourself most of the day as I did, in order to explore the area properly, both close-up and further away. I was quite amazed to find that I could actually find peaceful areas away from the crowds and the incessant hawkers, just by hiking a little ways away into the desert. And also the different lighting from morning to midday to dusk (and also with the range from clouds to full sun as was the case on the day I visited) creates a real range of different photographic opportunities.

Aswan:

From Cairo, I took a train south down the **Nile River**, to what is referred to as **Upper Egypt**; which includes **Aswan** as well as the city of **Luxor,** which I'll talk about next. Aswan is an interesting city well worth visiting along the Nile River, with a plethora of ancient sites and other things to see. The views of the Nile River, particularly at sunset, are absolutely exquisite, and the city has a main bazaar that is fun to walk down and soak up the bustle and lively character of Egyptian culture outside of the more westernized Cairo. The **Aswan Dam**, a dam along the Nile River upstream from the city of Aswan, is one of those things that you're supposed to see, as it creates **Lake Nasser**, the third largest reservoir in the world. I saw it as part of a day tour that included other sites around Aswan. As such it was worth a visit, though honestly I wouldn't go out of your way to see it otherwise. It could have easily been any reservoir as seen from Nevada or elsewhere in the American southwest: a dam and a lake set in a stark desert setting. The vastness of the lake isn't actually apparent, because it's a very long, thin reservoir and so you don't see the vast majority of it from the dam.

Instead, I would highly recommend setting aside ample time to explore the astounding and incredibly beautiful **Philae Temple**, situated on an island in the Nile River, downstream from the Aswan Dam (and thus closer to the city of Aswan). The current location is actually different from its original location, which was flooded in the course of the damming of the Nile River. The Philae Temple includes a complex of several different buildings, and features an impressive display of Egyptian hieroglyphs on both the larger, grand scale and the smaller, more intricate scale. I would rank the Philea Temple as the number one site to make sure to visit when visiting Aswan.

Luxor:

Luxor, also on the Nile, is home to many of the most interesting, and most famous ancient Egyptian sites, including the **Karnak Temple**, within the city of Luxor itself, as well as the **Valley of the Kings** and **Valley of the Queens**, located in the desert nearby. The Valley of the Kings is where the **Egyptian pharaohs**, such as **Tutankhamen, Ramses, Seti** and others were entombed. Their wives were entombed nearby at the Valley of the Queens. As such, Luxor is absolutely steeped in the ancient history of Egypt, with many other ancient monuments scattered throughout the area. Luxor is a medium-sized city on the Nile River, not so different from Aswan, though certainly more touristy. It's well worth a visit both for the remarkable ancient sites, as well as exploring the city itself, including its atmospheric covered market area.

Dakhla Oasis:

The **Dakhla Oasis** is situated around the ancient town of **Mut**. Getting there from **Luxor** was no easy task, as there are no buses or trains that cover the six-hour journey, since there's virtually nothing in the area in-between! Buses do, however, connect this area and the other nearby oases with **Cairo** directly, in a north-south route. In order to get there from Luxor, I had to organize a shared taxi ride with several other people that I met at the hotel where I was staying in Luxor. Between the four of us, we ended up paying about 25 dollars each for the ride. Considering the vast expanse of lifeless desert we passed through in order to get there, this was a small price to pay. (Kudos to our brave taxi driver, who had never driven the route before.)

We stayed at one of the many amazing desert camps at the edge of the oasis, away from the main town area, this one with its own hot springs. The desert landscapes there are absolutely stunning and well worth the trip out there, whichever route you end up taking. And there weren't many other foreign travelers around. Make sure to visit the remarkably well-preserved remains of the Islamic fortified town of **Al Qasr**, built in the 12th century.

Bahariya Oasis:

I didn't spend much time in the **Bahariya Oasis**, but got enough of a taste to know that it's definitely worth visiting. I stayed one night at a guest house in the main town of **el-Bawiti;** and then did an overnight jeep excursion into the **White Desert** for one night. The desert landscapes were absolutely, indescribably beautiful beyond what I could have imagined, with smooth, undulating dunes creating artistic patterns as far as the eye could see, mixed with strange rock formations poking abruptly up out of the sand. And despite being the closest of the oases to Cairo, we saw only one other tourist vehicle out there. If you want to see something really amazing, as well as take a dip in some crystal clear pools in the middle of the desert, ask your tour guide to take you to the **Magic Springs**, a tiny oasis in the midst of the bone-dry desert.

Chapter 15—*Thailand*

I spent 2 ½ months in Thailand in 2007-2008. I didn't see as much as you might expect in that period of time, since I tend to stay in places for a while, often a week or more. But hey, no big rush when you're relaxing in tropical paradise! I visited three islands, none of them very well known or touristy; as well as ventured inland to the northern part of the country.

Bangkok:

To my surprise, I really loved **Bangkok**. I found it to be an interesting mix of past and future, of authentic Asian culture and modern conveniences. You can find the old-style markets, dark and dusty mazes of countless booths and stalls filled with everything imaginable, from weird-looking foods to jeans to electronics and much more. And then you can also visit clean, high-tech malls that put the malls in the U.S. to shame. I don't have any super secret insider tips on places to explore in Bangkok, as I didn't spend a lot of time there, and visited the usual tourist spots; such as the **Grand Palace** and the **Sleeping Buddha**, both of which are recommended. I did a fair amount of aimless wandering, which is of course always a good way to explore.

I stayed in the backpacker's haven of the **Khao San Road** area, which is a fun and conveniently located part of town for budget travelers. If you don't want to be right in the middle of the noise and all-night partying (actually the thumping music shut down at 2am, which was a relief the one time I stayed right on Khao San Road, right over a club) then there are places to stay nearby that are within a few minutes walk of Khao San Road itself. I managed to find a room for as cheap as 100 baht, or about $3. It was tiny and basic, but you can't beat that price. There are also nicer hotels within the Khao San Road area;

or, of course, you can spend as much as you like at one of the fancier hotels elsewhere in the city. In short, I would recommend leaving at least a few days to explore Bangkok, as there's a lot to see, it isn't expensive, the hassle there isn't bad compared to some other large cities around the world, and it's a fun place to explore.

Ayutthaya:

I highly recommend visiting **Ayutthaya**, an island in the middle of the **Chao Phraya River**, just a few hours north of Bangkok, and a UNESCO World Heritage site. It was the former capital of Thailand (actually Siam) from 1350-1767 when it was captured by the Burmese and destroyed. Not all of it was destroyed however, and the island is littered with the ruins of temples and other buildings, some of which are fairly intact. It's a great place to rent a bicycle and just spend an entire day with map and camera in hand, biking from one temple to another soaking up the ancient history. It makes a convenient stopover if you're headed to points further north, such as **Chiang Mai** or **Pai** (both of which I'll review below).

Chiang Mai:

Chiang Mai is a lovely little city, with a lot to see and do. The main tourist area is in the historical area, which is within a moated and walled section at the center of the city. This entire area is highly touristy, more so than I expected, which undoubtedly dilutes the experience quite a bit. But it's still a fun place to walk around, shop, eat out at the wide selection of restaurants, take a Thai cooking class, learn Thai massage, etc.; and it also makes a good base from which to explore other parts of the city. I was there for the **Loy Krathong** festival, which marks the end of the monsoon season. I highly recommend seeing this spectacular event there if you get the chance; in which fireworks are in abundance, the river is filled with floating candles, and the night sky is filled with floating paper lanterns. It's a good thing it's right after monsoon when things are nice and wet, because this festival would be a major fire hazard otherwise! And make sure to see **Wat Phrathat Doi Suthep,** an elaborately decorated temple perched atop a mountain overlooking the city.

Pai:

I'm not exaggerating when I say that **Pai** may very well be the most touristy place I've seen in all my travels; at least in terms of budget travelers. The entire town seems to have been set up to accommodate budget backpackers. The center of town is a series of criss-crossed roads, in which virtually every business is either a guest house, hotel, restaurant, gift shop, music store or something else catering to backpackers. Almost all of the restaurants were blasting western style music. If you're looking for anything resembling an authentic Thai experience, this isn't the place to go.

However, that said, it's still a pleasant little town, set in the midst of an absolutely idyllic valley with some great exploring opportunities. At least there's a great selection of restaurants, and you'll probably meet a fellow traveler or two. I rented a bicycle and biked off down some country roads in which I managed to get away from the overwhelming tourist scene. And I really loved my room there, my own little private wooden cabin situated under some trees, right near the town center, for only about $5 a night. If I could remember the name of the lovely place I would mention it here, but that was over four years ago...sorry!

So I don't mean to say to avoid Pai necessarily. Just don't go there if you're looking for a rich cultural Thai experience, because you won't find it. But you will most likely enjoy your time there, as long as you don't mind eating your **pad thai** to the sounds of the Smashing Pumpkins blasting in your ears, or some other American band.

Ko Mak:

Ko Mak is a small island in the southeastern part of the country near the Cambodian border (which you can get to from the small town of **Trat**), and also right next to the much more popular island of **Ko Chang**, which has become a major destination for backpackers. I didn't stop at Ko Chang, instead taking the boat straight to Ko Mak. But I can say that Ko Mak is definitely a lovely little island and a great place to relax on the beach and read a book in a hammock. There's no nightlife whatsoever, and barely even anything resembling a town. There are a few nicer resorts on the island, as well as an assortment of budget-style bamboo hut resorts, one of which I stayed in. The only restaurants seemed to be the ones that went along with the resorts. My hut was, once again, in the $5-6 range, and quite nice, with its own bathroom, balcony and hammock. I spent the days walking up and down the various beaches, swimming, bicycling around the island, reading and not much else, since there wasn't much else to do. But hey, what else do you need?

Ko Kood:

Ko Kood is a larger island that's the third island in the chain after Ko Chang and Ko Mak. I didn't get the chance to fully explore it, as I got sick there and spent most of the time in my room. But it definitely seemed like it had potential, and it was certainly well off the tourist trail, at the time anyway. I did manage to get out one day in which I went on a hike through the jungle to a waterfall that was a fun adventure. It sounded as if there was a lot more jungle exploring to be done, and also more beaches to find, which I'll have to do the next time I go back. And even though I didn't visit the more popular island of Ko Chang at the time, I would probably check it out the next time for contrast; which gives you three worthwhile islands to explore all right near each other.

Ko Phayam:

Ko Phayam was really the highlight of my trip to Thailand. It is by no means undiscovered, as I found out about it from my Lonely Planet guidebook. But it doesn't get much attention despite being a great little island with some nice beaches, a pleasant little village, some good snorkeling and beautiful jungle to explore. There's just the one little village where the ferry boat docks, and the rest of the island is accessed by narrow cement paths navigated by motorcycles, as there are no cars on the island.

You can get there from the town of Ranong. And just for the sake of confusion, Ko Phayam island is the next island past **Ko Chang**. *But no, not the previously-mentioned Ko Chang!* There are two Ko Chang islands in Thailand, and this one is on the exact opposite side of the country, on the Andaman Sea and near the border with Myanmar. Again, I didn't visit that Ko Chang either. But I heard good things about it and would have visited if I could have gone there directly from Ko Phayam. But instead it required going back to the town of Ranong first, taking a separate boat and retracing your steps back to Ko Chang. Apparently it's even more rustic than Ko Phayam, with no roads or vehicles at all, but only hiking trails to get around the island. So it's worth looking further into and perhaps visiting while you're in that part of the country, as long as you're not attached to many modern conveniences.

Chapter 16—*The Philippines*

I spent three weeks in the Philippines in October of 2010. My aim was to spend most of my time on the island of **Palawan,** which I'd heard a lot of good things about; one being that it wasn't overly touristy yet despite having a lot to see. I only spent two nights in a hotel on the edge of **Manila,** and didn't even go into the main part of the city, so I won't be reviewing Manila at all. All three places I will review here are on the island of Palawan. The most notable attraction in Palawan is the **Puerto Princesa Subterranean River National Park** (also known as the **Puerto Princesa Underground River**), which is a UNESCO World Heritage site and is one of the declared winners of the **New 7 Wonders of Nature** (all seven winners haven't yet been declared, as of February 2012). Despite the name, it actually isn't in **Puerto Princesa,** but nearer to the town of **Sabang,** so look for the review there. Overall, I would highly recommend the region of Palawan if you're looking at visiting the Philippines, are seeking great beaches and beautiful landscapes, a wide variety of outdoor activities, yet aren't interested in immersing yourself in the crowds, noise and hassle of somewhere that's been overrun by tourism.

Puerto Princesa:

Puerto Princesa is the largest city (more of a town actually) on the island of Palawan, and where you will almost certainly fly into if you fly there. I enjoyed it and would recommend spending a couple of days there just to explore and get a feel for the place, even though there aren't any particularly notable attractions. It was a much mellower place to get acquainted with the Philippines than Manila. I stayed at the **Banwa Art House**, which I highly recommend as a place to stay. It's a completely wooden structure, artistically constructed as the name implies, with an amazing balcony area where people can hang out and work on the computer, read, play games, as well as order meals. There's a dorm room with sturdy wooden bunk beds, as well as private rooms.

As mentioned, there wasn't a whole lot in particular to do in Puerto Princesa, other than walk around the town, do a little shopping, find a good restaurant or two, walk down to the waterfront, etc. I met someone at the Banwa Art House and we went searching for a beach that was mentioned in the guidebook, but weren't overly impressed by it. So there's no need to plan on spending too long here, but it's a good place to unwind for a day or two before heading to the more interesting parts of the island.

Sabang:

Sabang is the nearest town to the **Puerto Princesa Underground River**, even though it's actually 30 miles (50 km) from Puerto Princesa, on the opposite side of the island of Palawan. You can get there an assortment of different ways, but the recommended form of public transportation is the **jeepney**. Jeepneys are large hum-vee type vehicles, relics of the U.S. presence in the Philippines during World War II, which have become the most popular form of public transportation in the Philippines. They are often very colorfully painted on the outside, and as expected tend to get overfilled, to the extent of carrying passengers as well as furniture and who-knows-what-else up on top.

To get to Sabang from Puerto Princesa by public transport, you'll first have to get yourself out to the main bus/jeepney station which is outside of Puerto Princesa a little ways. This will likely involve utilizing one of the other most popular vehicles in the Philippines—the funny-looking tricycles, which are essentially a motorcycle with a strange contraption built around it, allowing three people (including the driver) and a little bit of luggage to be carried at the same time.

The trip from Puerto Princesa to Sabang will take several hours, despite being only thirty miles (I didn't know it was that short of a distance, but had assumed it was more like a hundred miles by how long it took). This is because, same as in India and most places in Asia, the public transportation tends to stop anywhere people need to get on or off. And then, you may have to get all that stuff up onto, or else off of the roof!

But once you get to Sabang you will be pleasantly surprised, as it's pretty much picture perfect tropical paradise. It's barely even a village, but consists of a long line of houses and shops situated along the main road, which ends abruptly at a circular parking area/turnaround right by the beach; and then you're there, amidst the gentle lapping of the ocean waves and the swaying of palm trees. The various resorts are all off to the right (when facing the water), so just hop off and head that way. I stayed at the last collection of huts about a ten minute walk down the path that goes just behind the beach. It was pretty much along the lines of other bamboo huts I've had elsewhere, about $7 for my own hut with private bathroom, mosquito netting over the bed, and a nice little balcony. They had their own restaurant, and the beach was just a few steps away.

There are two different ways to get to the Underground River itself, which is about three miles north of the town of Sabang. Either you can take one of the boats that go regularly back and forth up the coast, ferrying tourists, or you can hike the trail through the jungle. Do as you wish of course, but I would highly recommend taking the jungle trail, which was about as interesting as the Underground River itself, if not more so. It's a winding path that goes up and down some steep hills and will take an hour or two. But you really can't get lost, and you get a real taste for the jungle, with monkeys swinging from the trees and the ever-present sounds of a million or so insects buzzing away in the background. I even saw a massive monitor lizard crawling slowly across the trail.

Once you arrive at the Underground River, whichever way you choose to get there, you will be greeted with a bit of a tourist frenzy, since it's a fairly popular attraction. You pay the fee of 150 PHP (about $3.50 USD) and then are given a hard hat and directed to where to wait for the next available boat to take you upstream along the river that will then go into the cave from which the river emerges. English-speaking guides accompany the small boats.

The Underground River is certainly impressive, but wasn't overly mind-blowing in my opinion; perhaps because I've been on other cave tours in California and elsewhere that had similar features. But nonetheless, it's absolutely worth making the trip there to see it, especially considering that Sabang is such a pleasant place to visit anyway. So I would give yourself at least a couple of days there, if not more, so that you have a day to devote to getting to the Underground River and back, and another day to just enjoy the beach and watch the palm trees swaying in the wind.

El Nido:

El Nido, at the far northern tip of the island of Palawan, is really the jewel of the island. Getting there can be a bit tricky since a good section of the road isn't paved; and if it's been raining lately, as was the case when I traveled there, that means it's mud. I went there direct from Sabang, but actually didn't make it in one day since I started late in the morning. I caught the first jeepney that came along, headed back towards Puerto Princesa, and then hopped out at the junction where the main highway heads north. Despite being only 15-20 miles, this took almost two hours. In leaving Sabang, we seemed to stop at every other house along the way to let people on or drop people off.

At the highway junction I then caught the next bus that came along, which took me north along the long sliver of the island of Palawan, to the town of **Roxas**. Arriving there late in the afternoon, I realized I wasn't even halfway to El Nido, and had better stop there for the night rather than risk doing part of the journey in the dark.

The next day I got up early and caught the next bus to El Nido, which took much of the day, and involved a lot of muddy, pot-holed roads. Finally we came to paved road, and shortly thereafter arrived in the picturesque little town of El Nido. Situated on a beautiful little bay, with various **tiny islands** visible off in the distance, it seemed like the perfect setting for a pirate movie of some sort.

Though there isn't too much happening in the tiny town of El Nido itself, there's a lot to see around the area, in particular relating to the many little **islands and islets** that can be seen off shore, and the many others that are further away. **Local boatmen** will take you on day trips out to the islands to swim, snorkel, find beautiful beaches on which to spend the afternoon, explore lagoons, etc. There are several prominently displayed travel agents that can plan a trip for you; or else just ask around.

Additionally, the bay itself that the town is nestled around is a good spot for swimming and lounging. And, if you take the path that heads to the north (go right when facing the ocean), it will take you up the coast, to beach after beach after beach. A great way to spend the day.

My favorite beach in the area, however, was in the other direction. I'd seen the beach from the bus on the day I arrived in El Nido. I took note of where it was, as it happened to be right where the muddy, gravelly road finally became paved (not the most reliable landmark, since this may have changed since then, but it worked at the time!). The beach was actually a little ways from the road, and it wasn't clear exactly how to get down to it. So I rented a mountain bike in town, and then biked about 30 minutes back up the main road. Sure enough, once I got to where the pavement stopped, I could see the gorgeous beach a little ways away, on the other side of a forest of waving palm trees. I looked around, and eventually found a small dirt path heading in that direction. I continued down the path by bicycle, and soon enough came to the beach, which more than met expectations. I locked my bike up under a tree and then continued walking along down the coast (heading south) which was a series of beaches that seemed never-ending. I never did find the "last" one so to speak, but simply turned around and headed back, leaving plenty more to be explored the next time I find myself in that part of the world.

Chapter 17—*Nepal*

I spent two weeks in **Nepal** in March, 2008, hiking the **Annapurna Base Camp** trek, also known as the **Annapurna Sanctuary**. I entered Nepal by bus from India in the southwestern part of the country, and then left that way as well, so I never went to

Kathmandu. Instead I went to **Pokhara**, third largest city in Nepal, stayed there for several days getting ready for the trek, and then started the trek not far out of the city.

Pokhara:

After three months spent traveling throughout India beforehand, arriving in **Pokhara** felt not unlike being dropped off suddenly in Switzerland. By comparison to the intense crowds, congestion and pollution of India, it was exquisitely clean, calm, tranquil, free of garbage, beggars, randomly placed animals (cows, pigs, dogs and monkeys that you see everywhere in India), and it was entirely hassle-free in terms of not having touts and hustlers trying to get you into their shops or into their rickshaws, etc. If you were to actually ask a Swiss their opinion, they might beg to differ. But all considering, Pokhara is a very pleasant, clean and easygoing little city set on a pretty lake and ringed by spectacular mountains; though not the taller snow-capped peaks of the Himalaya which are just out of sight.

Pokhara is undoubtedly touristy, as it is the hub for outdoors enthusiasts and adventurers of all types, getting prepared for, or else coming back from trekking in the **Himalaya Mountains**, and a wide variety of other adventure activities that can be done in the area. The main tourist center along the lake is lined with assorted guest houses, restaurants, gift shops, outdoors stores, travel agents—all the usual tourist necessities one would expect to find. It's a fun place to stroll around and people-watch, as long as you don't mind the fact that a good percentage of those people aren't from Nepal. You can rent boats to take out on the lake, and go for a refreshing swim. Or rent a bicycle to explore other parts of the city. All in all, it's a fun place to hang out for a few days or longer, and take care of all the necessary preparations for trekking up into some of the highest mountains in the world.

The Annapurna Base Camp Trek/Annapurna Sanctuary:

There are two completely separate treks associated with the **Annapurna** region. (Actually there are undoubtedly more than that with various alternate routes, but two main ones that most people embark on.) The **Annapurna Circuit Trek** is actually the most popular trek in Nepal. This *isn't* the trek that I did in 2008 (though I hope to do it the next time I visit Nepal). The Annapurna Circuit trek makes a huge loop AROUND Mt. Annapurna, and takes several weeks to complete. That trek does *not* go to the Annapurna Base Camp (also known as **ABC**).

The **Annapurna Sanctuary trek** on the other hand, which is the one that I did, instead goes in a straight line (well, more or less) up to the **Annapurna Base Camp** and back, and can be done in about a week. I hiked it with a friend who had done it before, and who then went on to hike the Annapurna Circuit trek afterwards. I would have loved to have joined him for that longer trek around the mountains, but had a plane to catch out of Delhi, India.

The Annapurna Sanctuary trek does not require any special equipment or know-how. I'm not a mountaineer, just a hiker and backpacker. The trek also doesn't require you to have your own porters (though you can hire them, and also a guide, if you prefer), or to bring your own gear such as a tent, stove, sleeping pad, etc.

Instead, there are lodges in various places along the trail, rather liberally placed, often in small villages but also in between, so that you can pick one based on however long you might want to hike for that day. They will also prepare your meals; and you can stop at other lodges along the way for lunch or else buy assorted snacks (like Snickers bars! I consumed at least three a day) at little shops in the villages. You can't easily lose your way, as you simply follow the main path that varies from a wide dirt hiking path, to a wider cobblestone path. When in doubt, just ask the locals for directions. There are a few junctions along the way, and you will want to bring a basic map in order to navigate at some points. But altogether it's a pretty straightforward venture. You will simply need warm clothing, water bottle, an extra blanket or sleeping bag just in case the lodge doesn't provide you with quite enough, or you get cold in the middle of the night, and the usual stuff you would need such as a toothbrush and toothpaste, a book or two, extra socks and underwear, sunscreen, sunglasses, sun hat, wool cap, moleskin for blisters, etc.

Keep in mind, however, that you WILL need to be in good shape. It is not a walk in the park. In fact, it involves one hell of a lot of elevation gain, because the beginning of the trail is at less than 3,000 feet, rising to 13,550 feet (4,130 meters) at the base camp. If you do the trek up there in four days, as we did, that means you're talking about a

2,500 foot elevation gain each day. (Going back takes less time, 2-3 days since, of course, it's downhill.)

The trek can technically be done any time of year. Earlier in my trip in India, before having done the trek, I spoke to some people who had done the trek in December, in the middle of a blizzard. This is not, however, recommended!! For one thing, you'll miss all the great views, not to mention be shivering cold the whole time. Instead, it's recommended to do the trek anytime from March to November. I did the trek starting in mind-March, which was actually a perfect time to do it. The mountains were all covered in white from the winter snows, but the weather was great, with sunny days and cool nights (it did get down around freezing up at the top). And there weren't too many other trekkers on the trail yet, since the trekking season was just beginning.

As for the scenic beauty you encounter along the way, there's nothing else like it; at least nothing I have yet to experience. The mountain views are absolutely spectacular, and hiking through the massive valleys, hopping over creeks on hanging bridges felt like being lost in an Indiana Jones movie. The views from the base camp itself are beyond description. We arrived late in the afternoon, amidst low hanging clouds that didn't allow us to see the mountains we were hiking in the middle of.

In the morning, with clear blue skies, we were treated with one of the most gorgeous settings imaginable. **Mt. Annapurna** isn't actually just one peak. There's **Annapurna 1** (the tallest at 26,545 feet/8,091 meters), **Annapurna 2**, **Annapurna 3**, **Annapurna 4**, **Annapurna South** and **Gangapurna**. Also in the area is **Hiunchuli**, **Machapuchare**, and many other snow-covered peaks. The Annapurna

Base Camp sits in a valley ringed by all of these peaks. Waking up to the pink glow of the rising sun shining onto the stark white of these mountains was a thrill like none other.

Chapter 18—*Singapore*

The tiny Asian island nation of **Singapore** (which actually consists of 63 different islands, off the southern tip of **Malaysia**) is a world apart from the Himalaya Mountains of Nepal, or from much of Asia for that matter; as it is an island not only geographically, but of wealth. It is one of the top five busiest ports in the world, the fourth-leading financial center in the world, and has the world's highest percentage of millionaire households.

Since I wasn't one of those millionaires, I stayed in a bunk in a hostel in the backpacker travelers area of **Little India**. It only seemed fitting since I was flying next to India. The area is centrally located and right near a subway stop, making it easy to get there from the airport.

I was in Singapore for just four days, and since prices for things there are higher than other places in Asia, I avoided the expensive attractions. I mostly spent my time exploring by walking around the city, or else taking the convenient and affordable subway system. Singapore is undoubtedly a fascinating place, a strange mix of the most modern conveniences and technology, with one of the most culturally diverse societies on the planet. And you can't complain about the weather, which averages somewhere in the 80s Fahrenheit (low 30s

Celsius) year-round. If I had to live in a large city, I can say that it's one I would certainly consider. Plus it's one of the busiest airports in the world, and so it makes a convenient stopover from and to other points in Asia. As long as you're flying in that direction, you might as well get off and explore for a few days.

Gabriel Morris is an author, photographer, world traveler, outdoors enthusiast and nature lover. He was born in Vancouver, Canada, raised in rural northern California and has also lived in Alaska, Hawaii, Oregon and Alberta, Canada. He has been traveling the world off and on for more than twenty years. He is author of *Kundalini and the Art of Being* (Station Hill Press, 2008), a gripping spiritual adventure story and cross-country hitchhiking travelogue; and of *Following My Thumb: A Decade of Unabashed Wanderlust* (Soul Rocks Books, 2012), a collection of 26 autobiographical travel tales from around the world. To see photos and videos of his world travels and read excerpts from his other writing, visit his website at: **Gabrieltraveler.com**.

Do you like to travel?

Or, do you simply wish that you could??

If you're interested in more writing by Gabriel Morris, his new book, titled *Following My Thumb: A Decade of Unabashed Wanderlust* (Soul Rocks Books, 2012) is a compilation of 26 autobiographical travel stories from 1990-2000. It chronicles his travels, tribulations, bumblings and ramblings throughout his late teens and 20s.

Tales of worldly wanderings and mishaps contained within its pages include: Hitchhiking the length of the U.K...Sleeping out on the streets of Paris...Getting lost in Denali National Park, Alaska...Getting mixed up with a wacky cult in Sedona, Arizona...Falling in (and out) of love with a fellow hitchhiker...Hiding in the nude from commando forest rangers while camping in the Hawaiian rainforest...Dodging tigers in the Indian jungle with two Israeli travelers, while awaiting the (supposedly) catastrophic effects of Y2K...and much more.

The book is fun, funny, adventurous and thought-provoking, as Gabriel searches for truth, purpose, excitement and good company while broke and on the road, but never lacking in creative solutions.

Following is the Foreword of *Following My Thumb: A Decade of Unabashed Wanderlust*...

Foreword...*The beginnings of a hitchhiker*

(early 1980s)

I first started hitchhiking when I was eight or nine years old. My parents were hippies in the '70s and '80s and we lived up a dirt road outside a small town in rural northern California. The school bus would take me five miles out of town and then drop me off at the bottom of our gravel road. From there it was a mile-and-a-half walk to our big cabin in the middle of the woods. For my short little legs following a long day at school, this seemed at times like an impossible trek.

But of course my dad thought it would build character (thirty years later, I'll admit it probably did) and my whimpering went unheeded. So what if there were a few hills to climb after a long day at school? When my dad was a kid, he'd biked halfway across Los Angeles to go to a school outside of his district, because he played trumpet in their school band. At least I didn't have to dodge noisy city traffic and breathe exhaust along the way, and then try to play a trumpet in tune. I was lucky to have clean mountain air to breathe, and the soothing sounds of nature to accompany my stroll.

So I trudged reluctantly home every day, creating little mind games to help keep me going. I would pretend I was on an explorer's expedition in a foreign land, searching for some kind of treasure along the way—maybe a coin or a hubcap, or even a Native American arrowhead. Or else I would pick a spot a ways down the road and tell myself that all I had to do was make it that far. When I'd made it to that spot, I would choose another point down the road and keep going, one short, boyish step at a time.

One day while walking home with my head down, halfway there and wondering if I was really going to make it this time or else, perhaps, end up curling up in the woods to take a nap, a car came down the road and pulled up alongside me. Occasionally I did get a ride, if my mom or dad happened to be coming home from work or if one of our immediate neighbors cruised by.

I lifted my head in expectation as the man rolled down his passenger window.

"Hey, kid, you look beat—you want a ride? I'm going on up the road to Richard's."

I didn't recognize him. He wasn't one of our neighbors or anyone I'd seen before. I considered hopping in—but then remembered my mom's caution about accepting rides from strangers. Well, he *knew* someone I knew. Richard was a friend of my dad's. But he was still technically a stranger, if a friendly one.

"Uh, no thanks," I said. "I'm not going much further." Only another long, hot, blistering mile or so.

"Alright kiddo, no problem—see ya later…" He continued down the road, leaving me in a cloud of dust.

This set me to thinking. I was really tired of walking this long way home every day after school. A quarter-mile would have been fine. Down our long driveway after a ride up the road was no problem at all. But a mile-and-a-half felt, at that moment at least, like cruel and unusual punishment. I wasn't going to do it. I wanted a ride, and I was willing to wait for it.

I had a good book in my backpack, so I sat down under a tree beside the road and started reading. It was warm and sunny and I found myself immediately happy not to be walking. I loved reading—so suddenly I was doing something that I loved, rather than hated. Why hadn't I thought of this earlier? I felt like that guy must have when he invented shoelaces—something so simple and obvious, yet brilliantly beneficial. Maybe this wouldn't make me rich. But it most certainly would improve my standard of living.

I reasoned that I could safely accept a ride from any person or car that I recognized and thus wasn't a true stranger. Expanding the criterion beyond our immediate neighbors and close family friends opened up the possibilities greatly, since dozens of people lived down our road, and my family knew most of them to some degree or another. After reading for a half-hour or so, a rusty old Toyota station wagon came clunking along towards me, trailed by the usual roiling cloud of dust. I recognized the car, although I wasn't quite sure who owned it. So I stood up and stuck out my thumb, just like I'd seen older guys doing while on family road trips. The car pulled over, and it was a neighbor that lived a little ways past us. His was a familiar face—good enough. I hopped in and got a ride all the way to the top of our driveway.

The following day after the bus had dropped me off I walked a quarter-mile up the gravel road and once again sat down in a shady patch of grass and started reading. When the first familiar car came along, I didn't even get up. I just looked up from my book and held my thumb high. The car pulled over. It was official—I was a hitchhiker.

Following My Thumb is available as both an e-book, and in paperback, which can be shipped worldwide. For more information visit:

http://gabrieltraveler.com

21244573R00066

Made in the USA
Middletown, DE
12 December 2018